ALDEBURGH

A Song of the Sea

ALDEBURGH
A Song of the Sea

TIM COATES

ANTIQUE COLLECTORS' CLUB

This book is dedicated to Bridget, Sam and Olly, Lydia, Amy and Rufus

ISBN: 978 1 85149 607 5

British Library Cataloguing-in-Publication Data
A catalogue record for this book is available from the British Library

The author and publisher gratefully acknowledge the permission granted to reproduce the copyright material in this book. Every effort has been made to trace copyright holders and to obtain their permission for the use of copyright material. The publisher apologises for any errors or omissions in the text and would be grateful if notified of any corrections that should be incorporated in future reprints or editions of this book.

Cover: *Victoria Parker-Jervis,* Aldeburgh Beach, 1992, oil on canvas, 58 x 83cm.
Reproduced by kind permission of the artist, courtesy of The Orwell Press.

Facing title page*: Derek Chambers*, South Lookout, etching, 41 x 30cm.
Reproduced by kind permission of the artist.

Title page: the statue of Snooks the doctor's dog, who for many years accompanied Dr Robin Acheson as he made his calls around Aldeburgh. He was called Snooks after the tinned fish snook (or snoek) from South Africa that was eaten during the war. He also had a tendency to eat pebbles, which led to more than one session under the surgeon's knife.

Endpapers: *Ken Hayes*, Aldeburgh Beach, 2013. Watercolour, 38 x 28cm.
Reproduced by kind permission of the artist

Printed in China
for the Antique Collectors' Club Ltd., Woodbridge, Suffolk, England

CONTENTS

Acknowledgements   8

CHAPTER 1:   Aldeburgh today – a sketch   10

CHAPTER 2:   Benjamin Britten and his legacy   26

CHAPTER 3:   The Aldeburgh Festival – Britten's legacy   46

CHAPTER 4:   Shape, shadow and form – the art of Aldeburgh   56

CHAPTER 5:   Writers and thinkers   68

CHAPTER 6:   Early history   82

CHAPTER 7:   Tudors   100

CHAPTER 8:   Carved stones and marsh spirits   114

CHAPTER 9:   Victorians and Edwardians   132

CHAPTER 10:   The Wentworths and the Garretts – dynasties and politics   150

CHAPTER 11:   Defence and war   166

CHAPTER 12:   Sea and life   182

CHAPTER 13:   The coastline and the future   194

Postscript   202

Index   204

Select bibliography   206

Jill Carver, Last Sun, Aldeburgh, 1994,
oil on canvas, 28 x 35.5cm.
Reproduced by kind permission of the artist.

ACKNOWLEDGEMENTS

It is a privilege to have been asked to write about Aldeburgh and has been a fascinating pleasure.

I am grateful to Diana Hughes and the trustees of the Aldeburgh Museum at the Moot Hall; Caroline Harding, Jude Brimmer and Dr Nick Clark of The Red House Library at the Britten–Pears Foundation; the librarians of the County Archive at the Suffolk Record Office, Ipswich; and the librarians of the British Library.

Thank you, too, to Mary and John James of the Aldeburgh Bookshop; Martin Whitaker of Browser's Bookshop in Woodbridge; Pam Parker of Flick & Son Estate Agents, Aldeburgh; the Mayor of Aldeburgh; the late Cyril Fry and his wife Shirley; Jules George; Richard Webster; the Aldeburgh and District Local History Society and Claude Cox, book dealer. Pat Ward, Alec Burwood and Hugo Parry Jones each spent time showing me places I would not have seen and telling me stories I would not have known. Many thanks, also, to Tom Miller-Jones, Tony Bone and all the people in and near Aldeburgh who have helped, sent material, advised and so kindly and generously co-operated and given encouragement. Thanks to all those at ACC who have helped with the book: Diana Steel, James Smith, Catherine Britton, Susannah Hecht, Kim Yarwood, Lynn Taylor, Tom Conway and Stephen Mackinlay. The truths have come from all these sources; any errors and inventions are my own.

Editor's note

The publishers of this book wish to express their gratitude to the many artists and photographers who have allowed their work to be reproduced in this volume. Unless stated otherwise, copyright for all works is held by the artists. Special thanks are due to Nick Clark and Caroline Harding of the Britten-Pears Foundation, Mary and John James of the Aldeburgh Bookshop, Sir Edward Greenwell and Andrew Knibbs of Aldeburgh Contemporary Arts.

Theronda Hoffman, Carnival, Aldeburgh, 2012, oil, 51 x 76cm.
Reproduced by kind permission of the artist.

CHAPTER 1:
ALDEBURGH TODAY
A SKETCH

Aldeburgh is a small town on the east coast of England. Unique, old and wind blown, it is a cultural refuge known throughout the world for its beach, its buildings and its astonishing music. Holidays for festivals and for families bring visitors all the year long to this isolated and ancient seafaring community.

For 7,000 years, since fishermen first anchored on the shingle beach at the 'Old Borough', the best way to come to and go from the town has been by boat. Edward FitzGerald, the eccentric Victorian poet, used to sail up and around from the River Deben at Woodbridge. He wrote that 'there is no sea like the Aldeburgh sea', an expression that visitors to the town will understand. Nor is there an English esplanade with such a variety of eccentric houses. To arrive from the sea, as only the lifeboat, the fishermen, or the breathless, brave, early morning bathers do now, is as colourful an approach as the light of the rising sun on the painted houses.

In the fourteenth century, Aldeburgh was, for a while, declared independent of the legislature of the King of England and answerable to the Pope. The town has also been physically isolated from its administering county, Suffolk, for longer than it has been part of it. Only in the last hundred years has there been a 'macadamised' road from Saxmundham and Snape to Aldeburgh. For forty years before that, there was a railway line – but the most scenic approaches by land are the footpaths, now rarely used, north and south of the Alde estuary. Visitors who wander along these routes today will find them accompanied by the most beautiful views.

The town has been closer to the sea and countries across it than it has been accessible to the 'South Folk' of England (the origin of the name 'Suffolk'). A contemporary explorer of Aldeburgh can discover the once adjoining but now 'lost' village of Hazelwood on the old 'sailors' path', a grassy vale that wends its way obscurely from Snape Bridge towards the edge of the secluded town. The new main road is too far from the river to take a traveller close to the Roman port and causeway that formed an old road to nearby Orford. Coming from the south, only a walker will use the same approach along the medieval sea dykes, built by Dutchmen to protect the sheep pasture, that Joseph Mallord William Turner used as a place to make sketches of Aldeburgh in the early 1800s. This path led to Slaughden ferry, with its bell to call the boatman over. From that position, England's great painter of the sea depicted the shipyard and the new Martello tower.

Mandy Walden, The Dancing Fish Came to Shore to see the Boats Stranded as Folks Slept On, watercolour, 20 x 20 cm. Reproduced by kind permission of the artist.

Jules George, Running Through the Snow, Aldeburgh Beach, 2007, oil on linen, 30 x 22cm. Reproduced by kind permission of the artist.

Most of the houses on the High Street and the sea front were built long before the Victorian housing developments of the late 1800s. The Brudenell Hotel and the terrace at the south end of Crag Path close to the telegraph cable were constructions of the family of Newson Garrett. They were built on land that had previously comprised ancient military defence and a fortress surveying the North Sea shipping. Aldeburgh is a promontory, which explains much about the military importance of both the beach and the position

of the church, with its views inland and to the sea lanes north and south.

Nowadays, Crag Path, running along the top of the beach, gives the town its recognisable character. From here, on the beach, night fishermen watch the sunrise that inspired and is so clearly evoked in Benjamin Britten's *Sea Interludes* from his first opera, *Peter Grimes*.

The houses, meanwhile, are not simply individual but often do not appear English at all. There is a strong Dutch flavour to their design, which shows how closely this working community has been influenced by its maritime neighbours.

Nobody better understood the many aspects of the character of the town than the poet George Crabbe (1754-1832), who was born here. While he wrote about the murkiest aspects of the poor fishing folk and their politics, Crabbe also witnessed the arrival of visitors who came solely to enjoy the attractions of the sea and the landscape. This stanza from *The Borough* was written two hundred years ago:

> Of our Amusements ask you?—We amuse
> Ourselves and friends with seaside walks and views,
> Or take a morning ride, a novel, or the news;
> Or, seeking nothing, glide about the street,
> And, so engaged, with various parties meet...

The town has added only a few attractions since those times. The town burgesses have resolutely resisted the temptations of commercial exploitation on the sea front adopted almost everywhere else, and, instead, Aldeburgh has become a town of festivals and cultural pleasures. This noble policy has had the added advantage of preventing the town from becoming a worthwhile financial investment. Instead, it nourishes good intentions and pleasant people.

Alan Bridges, Crag Path, watercolour.
Reproduced by kind permission of the artist.

Of all these activities, the most famous and that which has the best international and historic reputation is the annual music festival and accompanying musical creativity, which originated with Benjamin Britten and Peter Pears after the Second World War. The variety of events, activities and associated educational work that are part of the festival organisation bring tens of thousands of people to Aldeburgh (and to the allied Snape Maltings site, just down the road) each year. The whole endeavour is rightly considered to have the greatest possible integrity and is an outstanding national attribute and advantage to Suffolk.

Within the warm embrace of the Aldeburgh Festival, and happy to be there, are a number of other literary and artistic festivals and events that take place throughout the year and make use of the buildings and the facilities in the town. Alongside several major international music events are the celebrations of food and drink, literature, poetry, summer theatre, documentary films and an August carnival that attracts families from all over East Anglia.

The Aldeburgh Literary Festival in particular has become one of the most prestigious events of its kind in the country and in its short existence has attracted speakers from the worlds of science, journalism and literature such as Richard Dawkins, P. D. James, Ian McEwan, Alan Bennett, Harold Pinter and many others.

Many people come to Aldeburgh to enjoy the yachting from Slaughden Quay, south of the town. Few, perhaps, realize the depth of history that surrounds the boatyard and clubhouses which are all that remain of this formerly thriving haven and its hundreds of years of boat-building. Records attest that Aldeburgh was once one of the leading boat-making towns in the country, with Sir Francis Drake's *Golden Hind* (*Pelican*) among its constructions. Not much is known about what preceded those boom times, but important naval and fishing vessels were built on this site for many centuries. Subsequently, Slaughden, of which only the shacks of the yard remain, would become another of the coast's 'lost' villages; the last house swept away in the storms of 1933 by the force of the ocean. In the 1850s, there was a proposal to breach the 2,000-year-old natural shingle bank between the Martello Tower and the old windmill (where huge sea defences have now been erected), but the idea was refused by Parliament. As a consequence, the River Alde still performs its extraordinary turn and runs south for fifteen miles to the coastguard's cottages at Shingle Street before its entry into the sea.

Just as the history of Slaughden is no longer obvious, nor do many people realise the role played by the marshland to the north of the town alongside the road to Thorpeness. The

John Bawtree

Haven, as it was known, was a second harbour for the town and a refuge for boats running south down the coast that needed to shelter from the powerful north winds, and which, if they lost control, would be run onto the sand banks off the south end of Aldeburgh beach. The entrance to the Haven was at the place now called 'Sluice Cottage', and the water was deep enough to take large vessels and provide shelter for them.

John Bawtree, Aldeburgh Boat Pond, 2001, oil on board, 25 x 30cm. Reproduced by kind permission of the artist.

Theronda Hoffman, Fireworks, Aldeburgh,
2012, oil, 51 x 76cm.
Reproduced by kind permission of the artist.

For those who find sailing boats on the sea or on the windy Alde too daunting, safe and sunny day boating is possible on all that remains of the Haven. At the north end of the former harbour is Thorpeness Meare, with its stone crocodiles and references to the stories of *Peter Pan*, written by J. M. Barrie when he visited the area. Real pirates and smugglers are part of the history of the town from the times when the east coast was running with gangs of dealers in contraband imports. If

there is treasure still buried – and there might well be – it could easily be in the shrubland and woods on the beach and behind the Haven and Thorpeness. Boatmen had a habit of hiding their valuable hauls and leaving them for later collection – and it is possible that some was left behind. Indeed, a great trove was discovered on Thorpeness beach in 1901 by Miss Lanyard. Such possibilities provide another reason for visiting the area.

Mandy Walden, All Set for a Busy Day, collagraph print with watercolour, 46 x 31cm. Reproduced by kind permission of the artist.

The Aldeburgh laundry was located on the north side of Fort Green and remained in operation until about 1938.

The popular beach lies between, at the northern end, the magnificent and powerful lifeboat station and, to the south, a remembrance of the Second World War, where what is now the lifeguard station (next to the Brudenell Hotel) was, in the 1940s, a steel and concrete bunker. This sturdy structure was built by tradesmen in the town and housed two enormous naval guns. At the time, the whole of the seafront and the road to Thorpeness was mined and defended in order to prevent a German beachhead being established for an enemy invasion.

Those who still seek a launderette for their holiday washing will find no comfort in the knowledge that there once was a laundry on this very site, but warfare and weather washed it away less than a hundred years ago and it has never been replaced. Only in Aldeburgh would the town allow a laundry on the sea front – but, in any case, it is no longer there. There is no shop, nowadays, on the old esplanade; none until, that is, one comes to the magical fishermen's huts beyond the lifeboat station, and these are among the country's more eccentric, but excellent, fishmongers. There are still boatbuilders in Aldeburgh, and – despite a major fire at one in 2010 – they continue to thrive and to contribute to the maritime activity of the town.

A fisherman's hut on the seafront.
Photograph by Tim Coates

The shops in the town, mostly on the length of the ancient High Street, are as smart and tasteful a collection as may be found anywhere. There are designer dresses and fine wines, delicatessens and jewellers as well as one of England's best bookshops, at the north end, and one of the most highly praised fish-and-chip shops at the south, on the way to old Slaughden and the barren wasteland past the Martello Tower.

George Crabbe understood the hierarchies of the isolated town and he also captured the social nature of the holidaymaking when he wrote:

> Cheerful meals the sunken spirits raise
> Cards, or the dance, wine, visiting or plays
> Soon as the season comes and crowds arrive
> To their superior rooms the wealthy drive
> Others look round for lodging snug and small

But he knew very well the reason why they had all come:

> Then may the poorest with the wealthy look
> On ocean, glorious page of nature's book
> May see its varying hues in every hour
> All softness then rising with all power
> As sleeping to invite or threatening
> Tis this which gives us all our choicest views
> Its waters heal and its shores amuse.

A hundred years after he wrote this, the Ward Lock tourist guide, written in about 1910, says:

> 'Amusements are of the quiet, open-air order. Restfulness and absence of excitement are characteristic of Aldeburgh. No steamboats call and no pier obstructs the sea view. The visitor can read his book or dream with no fear of disturbance by beach minstrels or vendors.'

Opposite:
Theronda Hoffman, Fish and Chips, Aldeburgh, 2012, mixed media, 27 x 38cm.
Reproduced by kind permission of the artist.

Right:
Jules George, Cod, Haddock or Plaice? (Fort Green), 2008, oil on linen, 30 x 24cm.
Reproduced by kind permission of the artist.

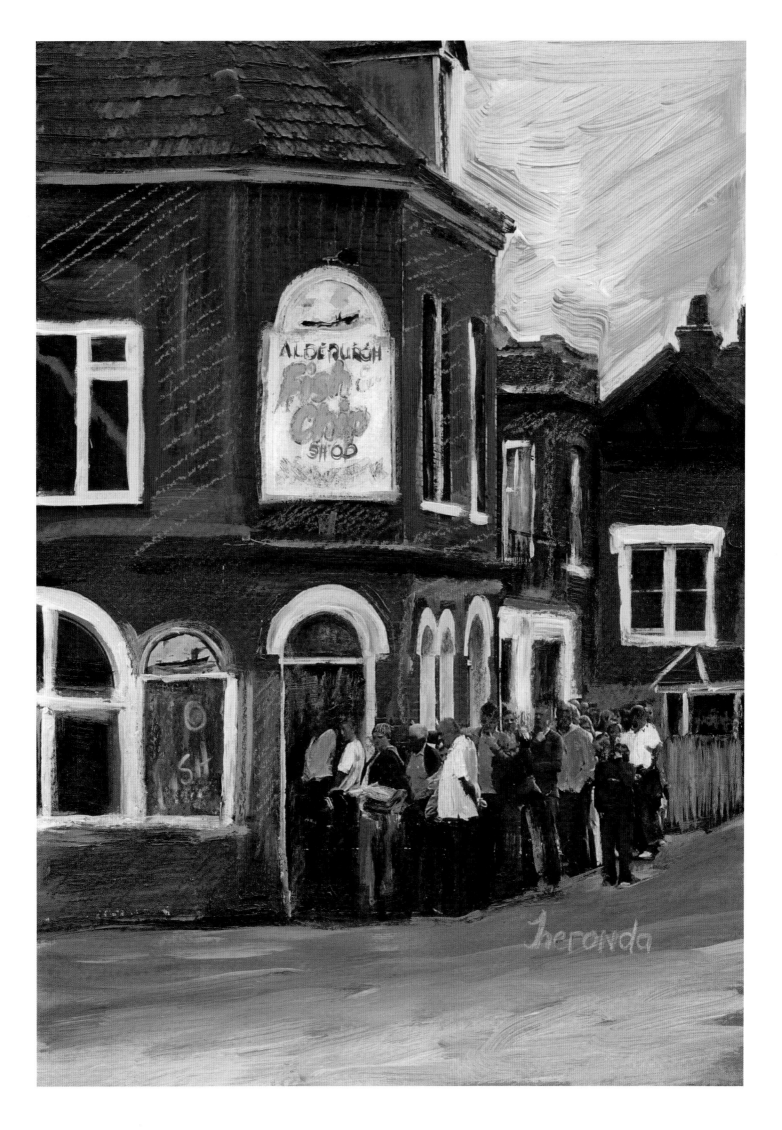

CHAPTER 2:
BENJAMIN BRITTEN
AND HIS LEGACY

In the early part of the twentieth century, who could possibly have imagined that Aldeburgh in Suffolk would become one of the most important and famous centres of classical music in the world?

The story starts in obscurity: Frank Bridge would be a long-forgotten musician if he had not also been a teacher at the Royal College of Music, where among his pupils in 1930 was a seventeen-year-old boy from Lowestoft called Benjamin Britten. The boy was a gifted and hard-working piano student, and a promising composer. Contemporary accounts depict a flustered, diligent child, anxious and serious, who was inspired by his teacher into the pursuit of accurate composition. Bridge insisted, above all, that what was written should be *exactly* what the student intended, whatever hard work was required to achieve that object. Thus, in the arts of harmony and orchestration, Benjamin Britten was highly and rigorously trained.

So schooled, Britten achieved a good reputation, both as a pianist and as a composer. However, his growing fame meant that some of his London friends selected and promoted him in a way that he might not have done himself. People much more outgoing than him prized his qualities, and he became something of a trophy for them.

In 1934, he found it was possible to make some money by writing film music and he was commissioned by the Post Office for a number of films advertising and explaining their services. In 1935 he worked on a project called *Night Mail* where he was introduced to a flamboyant young public schoolmaster called Wystan Auden.

W. H. Auden was five years older than Benjamin Britten but very quickly made the young man part of his 'set', recognizing his genuine talent as a composer and his possibilities as a friend. He also found the young boy attractive and vulnerable. The film *Night Mail*, released by the GPO in 1936, has Britten's musical score to words of Auden's poem:

> 'This is the Night Mail crossing the border,
> Bringing the cheque and the postal order,
> Letters for the rich, letters for the poor,
> The shop at the corner and the girl next door.
> Pulling up Beattock, a steady climb:
> The gradient's against her, but she's on time.'

Britten's domestic circumstances were still quite sheltered: he lived in London with his sister, loved going to watch Disney films, and his theatrical tastes were very much inclined towards satirical productions such as a staged version of *1066 and All That.* But his musical heroes were sophisticated and advanced: when Alban Berg died at Christmas in 1935 he wrote 'I feel it is a real and terrible tragedy from which the world will take long to recover... the real musicians are few and far between aren't they? Apart from the Bergs, Stravinsky, Schonberg and Bridges, one is a bit stumped for names isn't one... Shostakovich – perhaps – possibly'. Of the English composers such as Vaughan Williams and his generation he was wholly dismissive. 'There is more music on one page of *Macbeth* [the Shostakovich opera] than in the whole of their "elegant" output', he wrote.

His moment of tragedy and transformation came in early 1937. He and his sister had moved to a flat in Finchley Road. Britten's diary at this time records that he felt enormously inferior to almost everyone he met, from Auden and his group, to all the people with whom he worked on film projects. Auden had decided to go to fight in the Spanish Civil War, leaving his friend in depressed circumstances.

Britten described their home as 'the coldest flat in London, built on top of nothing, with nothing on either side of it'. His sister Beth came down with a terrible cold which developed into pneumonia; Ben also fell ill, so their mother came to look after them both. Inevitably, she too became seriously ill, and on the morning of Saturday 30 January, she died. 'So I lose the grandest mother a person could possibly have', he wrote in his diary. 'I only hope she realized that I felt like it. Nothing one can do eases the terrible ache that one feels – O God Almighty – '. It was a terrible, sudden event.

Kenneth Hari, W. H. Auden, My Adopted Father, 1968, graphite on paper, 60 x 75cm. In the 1930s Britten became part of Auden's artistic set, a move that gave him independence but inevitably changed his relationships with older friends such as Frank Bridge. Thirty years later Auden was painted by the young American artist Kenneth Hari who said 'Auden changed my life. He said my portraits should serve as a unification of man, not as decorative ornaments. It opened doors for me.' Reproduced by kind permission of the artist.

With the money left to him by his mother, Benjamin Britten searched for a place in which to live outside London. He and Frank Bridge scoured the county of Suffolk and came across the ruin of the old white flour mill at Snape. Ben intended that he and his composer friend Lennox Berkeley should live there and it would be a place for them both to compose. This was the mill formerly belonging to a Mr Hudson in which the fertilizing properties of the local stone Coprolite had been discovered, the profits from which had in turn helped to fund the building of Snape Maltings – but neither of them understood the significance of that!

Marjorie Fass, a friend of Frank Bridge wrote: 'I know he [Benjamin] is in a mental muddle about a great deal and dreads the future. He really hates growing up and away from a very happy childhood that ended only with his mother's death last Christmas.' Yet, at the same time, the influence of Auden and his circle made Benjamin Britten seek musical independence, and this inevitably irritated Frank Bridge and his close friends. That same Marjorie Fass wrote of Bridge: '[Frank] muttered that never again would he try and help Benjy with his work ... the thing that is bad for him is that he is meeting brilliant people who are not brilliant in music but in their own sphere.' Britten was writing songs to the words of Auden, and those of Auden's friend Christopher Isherwood, and he was reluctant to accept the modifications that Frank Bridge proposed.

Work started to convert the old mill at Snape into a house for music. The young composer wrote in his diary, 'The country is heavenly and the view from the Mill superb. As I go to bed the noise of the birds is deafening – Cuckoo, Nightingale, Sand Piper and Shell Drake. Mr Blowers the inn keeper from Sotterley, which we knew so well when at Lowestoft, keeps the Pub here.'

Hudson's flour mill at Snape in the 1930s. The mill was in use until only a few years before Britten bought it. Photographer unknown.
Reproduced courtesy of the Britten-Pears Foundation.

Notwithstanding his changing relationship with his mentor, the major work that he completed at this time was 'Variations on a Theme of Frank Bridge' for which the teacher expressed his most profound gratitude and pride.

Despite the acquisition of his Suffolk property, Britten still needed somewhere to stay when he was in London, and he moved into a flat in Earl's Court with another new friend called Peter Pears, a young musician who was trying to establish himself as a singer. Three years older than Britten, the descriptions of Peter Pears of that time are of a good-looking young man: quiet, inward, dignified but reticent in character. It is said that outwardly he gave little of his own mind. He came from a diplomatic family and his Englishness showed in his lasting pride at having played cricket at the Oval in London in his schooldays.

Pears' singing talent was late developing and was grounded in sheer hard work as he strove to develop his tenor voice into a unique sound. He first worked with Benjamin Britten for a BBC broadcast in 1937 and shortly afterwards went to America on tour with a group called the New English Singers.

In 1938 Benjamin Britten was invited to write a piano concerto for the BBC promenade concerts in which he would be the soloist. It was not yet a break into fame, but it was a step in that direction. In fact the concerto was not a great success. Frank Bridge was disappointed but was careful not to say so. His feeling was that Britten was confused by the influences he was under and not yet sufficiently strong to make the long sustained statement that such a work needed. Nevertheless, the major music critics in the national newspapers described Britten's work as important if not yet mature, and it was clear his reputation was growing.

The good luck note sent to Britten by W. H. Auden on the night of the first performance was 'Vive la musique: A bas les femmes' ('Long live music: down with women'). In contrast to Frank Bridge, Auden and his friends were vociferous in praising their protégé.

At this time, Aaron Copland, the American composer, was in England and Britten invited him to stay in Snape for a visit. Among the works Copland had with him was his draft score of an opera for schools called *The Second Hurricane*. Britten's curiosity about this work was enhanced by his observation that no English composer had written a serious and successful popular opera since the time of Purcell. There was a strong reaction against the music hall operettas of the nineteenth century; the world had been changed so much by the Great War.

By the end of the 1930s it was apparent that an international conflict in Europe was inevitable. Auden and Christopher Isherwood left for America and Britten and Peter Pears decided to follow them in April 1939. They had no plans to stay for a long time – it was a journey made by young men without commitments or responsibilities except to themselves and what they wanted to do. Britten wrote to Aaron Copland that they would stay as long their money lasted. Although Britten enjoyed living in Snape he had not yet made the connection to Aldeburgh that was to be so important to his life and legacy.

During April 1939 the Territorial Army began recruiting in Suffolk in order to bring their establishment up to the numbers needed for war. The expectation was that men of military age would be called up to fight in a British Expeditionary Force in Europe, as had happened in 1914. In less than a month more than 2000 men were recruited into the Suffolk Territorial Army, the largest number of volunteers of any English county.

Chrissy Norman, The Make Up Case, etching, 10 x 20cm. Reproduced by kind permission of the artist.

In America the two young musicians were encouraged by their friends to stay out of the fighting. Auden told them that 'my position, (as an artist), forbids me to act as a combatant in any war'. Aaron Copland wrote in a letter to Britten: 'I think you absolutely owe it to England to stay here; after all anyone can shoot a gun - but how many can write music like you?' Most people in England would have disagreed profoundly with those views. There was an overwhelming sense of duty to fight against German fascism and the domination of the Nazi regime as it spread across Europe. Moreover most people, rich or poor, did not have the option to travel abroad at this time and, in so doing, avoid the military activity that seemed to be so inevitable. Nor would many of them have wanted to do so.

In the spring of 1941 Britten and Pears drove across America in the hope that by crossing the border into Mexico they could then return with the status of permanent immigrants. Yet it was at this moment that a transformation took place which affected the history of Aldeburgh profoundly.

The Listener, the BBC journal, published an article by E. M. Forster about the Aldeburgh poet George Crabbe, and a copy of the magazine came into the hands of Britten and Pears in San Francisco. Forster wrote about Crabbe's landscape of 'an estuary, saltish commons and the marsh birds crying.'

In the following days Britten found a copy of Crabbe's poems and read them for the first time. The melancholy description of the seascape and village life was so evocative to him that it created not just severe homesickness, but an identification of the musical role he could and should play. Crabbe's work could be perceived as distressing to an upstanding native of Aldeburgh who might view it as a bleak presentation of a place to be proud of; but to a visitor, an outsider, a realist, Crabbe writes of a world which is plausible among the damp mudflats.

'Peter Grimes' is part of a longer narrative poem of 1810 by Crabbe entitled 'The Borough', and is the tale of a man who lives on a small boat and earns a living from the sea. In succession Grimes kills his old father and then three apprentices whom he has hired for the sole purpose of torturing, it seems. It is as dark, bleak and cruel a story as can be found, made worse by its credibility and realistic descriptions. Aside from Grimes and his victims there are no other named characters in the poem, but there is a role played both by the women villagers and by the burghers who undergo a succession of reactions, from horror to a final disgusted pity for the man. Even visitors to the town are depicted:

> 'Summer lodgers were again come down;
> These, idly curious, with their glasses spied
> The ships in bay as anchor'd for the tide
> The river's craft – the bustle of the quay –
> And sea port views, which landmen love to see.
>
> One, up the river, had a man and boat
> Seen day by day....'

This man who has been 'seen day by day' is Peter Grimes, who has begun to encounter the ghosts of his victims, and has become in his turn the victim of the guilt they induce in him. He blames his father for this torture saying that his pleasure is 'to plague and torture thus an only son'.

The whole poem of 375 lines is totally engaging – the events of the story it tells are horrifyingly compelling, but relentless in their gloom:

> 'Here, dull and helpless, he'd lie down and trace
> How sidelong crabs scrawled their crooked race
> Or sadly listen to the tuneless cry

Of fishing gull or clanging golden eye
What time the sea birds to the marsh would come
And the loud bittern from the bull rush home
Gave from the salt ditch side the bellowing boom:
He nursed the feelings these dull scenes produce'

One wonders why, out of all the words written about Suffolk and England, it was these that at this precise moment that made Benjamin Britten feel so homesick for Aldeburgh; but that is exactly what happened. This poem by George Crabbe, which in its own very particular way describes so intimately the Borough, its inhabitants, its conflicts, its seascape and its marshy countryside, had turned Britten and Pears in their tracks and gave them an urgent drive to return to the country they had so readily abandoned to its wartime fate. In an instant, they gave up their attempt to become American citizens and sought the first boat home. Who knows what powers of guilt, perhaps, or sadness, were released to make such a change, but it is a moment upon which much turned. In 1942 the Russian-born conductor and composer Serge Koussevitsky, whom Britten had come to know during his time in America, paid Benjamin Britten one thousand dollars to write the opera of the story of Peter Grimes and dedicate it to the memory of his wife who had recently died.

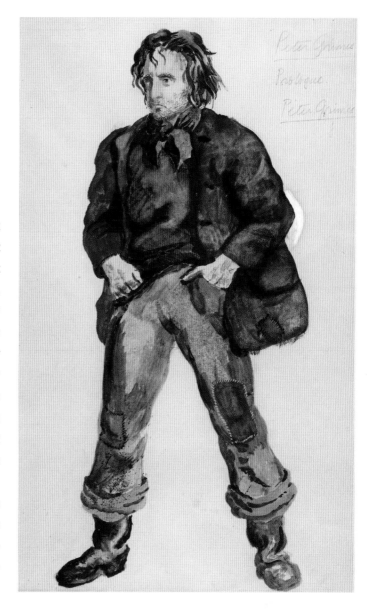

Costume design for *Peter Grimes*, Sadler's Wells, June 1945. Designer: Kenneth Green. Reproduced by permission of the estate of Kenneth Green, courtesy of the Britten-Pears Foundation.

Where English opera had previously faltered into the boisterous amusements of Gilbert and Sullivan, now young Benjamin Britten, the great musical craftsman, found the ingredients to re-create in operatic form the melancholy realism of George Crabbe, and the town of Crabbe's childhood.

Yet, at the same time, one could readily predict that the people of the town would not appreciate such an invention: they didn't like Crabbe, cowardly pacifists, outsiders, childish spoilt men who lived together, or modern music. Furthermore, they didn't want to be told that the most recognizable characters of their town were its solitary lunatics, vengeful Aldermen, gossiping women and the brutal demons that inhabit the river. Of course they didn't: who would? The uncomfortable conflict between composer and townsfolk was bound to be so.

'We, of Swallow as a monster, speak,
A hard bad man, who prey'd upon the weak.'

'Peter Grimes' the poem is about Aldeburgh, but the story of the opera of the same name is quite different. Montagu Slater, who was the librettist asked by Benjamin Britten to write the work, took characters from the other sections of 'The Borough' and changed the nature and personality of Grimes completely. In the opera, Grimes is harassed by the people of the town and is a victimised man, pushed out and rejected by them. In the poem he is plainly evil and is wholly guilty of multiple unprovoked murders; the town is an innocent witness to his crimes. Many of the characters of the libretto are inventions of Slater and Britten and not of George Crabbe. In the opera, Swallow is the pompous town lawyer who accuses Peter Grimes of murder in the name of the Borough. In the poem his name appears not within the story of Peter Grimes, but in another early section of *The Borough* in which Crabbe calls him 'a monster who prey'd upon the weak.' Ellen Orford, who in Crabbe's stories of the Borough is a blind old woman with a long history of lovers and children, is transformed into a completely new character in the opera, as Grimes' confidante and friend. However, the main difference between the poem and the opera is that the former centres on Grimes and the sea, and the landscape and the town are a backdrop; in the opera, the town and the man are equal characters in conflict.

Mandy Walden, Come to the Town Steps to see the Fishes Dance, collagraph print with watercolour, 34 x 34cm. Reproduced by kind permission of the artist.

So *Peter Grimes* became, for Britten, the portrait of a man cast out by his town in a way that Crabbe did not intend. The opera is most certainly Benjamin Britten's creation; it speaks of Aldeburgh clearly and famously as the villain of the drama. The town is a caricature.

If the people who lived there might reasonably have disliked the way that Crabbe had described them in 1816, the people of Aldeburgh in 1945 had much greater reason to object, if they wished, to the way Britten portrayed their heritage. Yet in its way the opera brought them fame and enduring fortune.

Peter Pears had become, on his return to England, one of the leading voices in the wartime Sadler's Wells opera company led by Joan Cross and Eric Crozier. It was these latter two who decided, in the face of the scepticism and objection of their colleagues, that *Peter Grimes* should be the opera that would re-launch their company when the war came to an end. Pears played the part of Grimes, Eric Crozier was the director and Joan Cross resigned her directorship of the opera company in order to play the part of Ellen Orford.

The performances at Sadler's Wells theatre were greeted with rapture from the first night and throughout the run. The website of the Royal Opera House records that 'Even the bus conductors used to shout "Next stop *Peter Grimes!* The murdering fisherman!" as they passed'. Both the artistic world and the popular press hailed Britten as a genius, and the success at Sadler's Wells meant *Peter Grimes* was scheduled for performances in the opera houses of Europe. It marked Benjamin Britten's breakthrough into national fame.

Around this time, Britten was invited to travel with Yehudi Menuhin, who was already one of the leading musicians of his time, to give concerts in German hospitals and reception centres that had recently been built in the concentration camps to care for the survivors at the end of the war. Britten was the accompanist. The experience was profound and he recorded that for ever after it affected the music that he wrote. He was thirty-two, and both he and Pears had by now achieved at least temporary financial liberation through their music.

Although Aldeburgh was in its way one of the main characters of *Peter Grimes*, Britten and Pears' lifelong relationship with the town did not really come about for a few more months. Britten was offered the opportunity of writing operas for Glyndebourne by its owner John Christie and his first work for him was *The Rape of Lucretia*. The sets were designed by the painter John Piper, who would go on to work with Britten on many future productions at Snape Maltings. If *Lucretia* had been more popular, it is possible that thereafter Britten would have written for Glyndebourne, but it was not. He was left uncomfortable with the country house elitism of Christie's Glyndebourne, and in any

case the endeavour was a financial failure. Britten was faced with the (not uncommon) critical phenomenon whereby an artist's second creation is treated less generously than his first one.

Nevertheless, Britten, Pears, Cross and Crozier were fired with self belief, and for their next operatic creation they returned to the theme of Suffolk and the sea. The opera *Albert Herring* was also first performed at Glyndebourne, but as its name suggests, it drew many of its ideas from life in a fishing town and the characters who lived there.

After its Glyndebourne opening, the 'English Opera Group' as these friends styled themselves, went on tour in Europe. *Albert Herring* had been booked for a performance at the first Holland Festival of Music after the war. *The Rape of Lucretia* was to be played in Lucerne and altogether there were twelve performances. It was a long and tiring tour and, much worse, resulted in a net loss of three thousand pounds.

John Piper, the backdrop for 'Loxford' in *Albert Herring*. The square is obviously the central square in Woodbridge with the town hall looking from the east, and Woodbridge church in the background. Set design by John Piper.
Reproduced by permission of the Piper estate, courtesy of the Britten-Pears Foundation.

Jennifer Hall, The Red House, etching and aquatint. Reproduced by kind permission of the artist.

'Why not make our own festival?' asked Peter Pears. 'A modest festival with a few friends? Why not have an Aldeburgh Festival? Why do we come to Switzerland to perform *Albert Herring*? Why can't we perform it at Aldeburgh?' It was a momentous conversation, recalled years later both by Eric Crozier and by Pears himself. The viability of the idea depended entirely upon whether the Jubilee Hall in Aldeburgh would seat 300 people, and although Britten and Pears had given a previous recital there, neither of them could remember how many tickets were sold nor how many empty seats there were. Nevertheless, they were determined to go ahead. In part, Britten's preference for a small fishing town as a new festival venue over places like Glyndebourne came from the same slightly socialist instinct of his artistic circle, with its dislike of the aristocratic establishment. But, of course, the idea of Aldeburgh as a centre for music is, as time has shown, a magical one, and this group of dynamic and idealistic young musicians were ready to make something special happen there.

Benjamin Britten sold the old flour mill in Snape and moved into Crag House on the seafront in Aldeburgh, only a few yards from the Jubilee Hall, and the group began preparations for the first Aldeburgh Festival, to be held in June 1948.

The English Opera Group raised one thousand pounds from their own funds, from a number of residents of the area and from the Arts Council, who put up half the initial amount.

Everything Benjamin Britten later did implies that his genuine intention was that the Aldeburgh festival would grow from and be part of the local community. It was a hard ambition to achieve: London at that time dominated almost every aspect of artistic life in England. If a professional performer was to play at the festival, it was almost inevitable that the person would come from London or overseas, and furthermore, it was assumed that the only audiences large enough to pay good fees were located in the capital.

Britten believed that not just a sufficient audience – but also a significant number of the performers should come from the local community – and he pursued that eccentric aim, although there was inevitable antagonism between the locals and the organisers. As the Festival's first chairman, Lady Cranbrook, later recalled, 'There were several difficulties at first. There was pacifism, God Save the King, and applause in church.' The Aldeburgh Festival was a local occasion from the outset, and yet very quickly its artistic integrity achieved the highest possible international reputation. In England an original creative artist not only has to conjure financial viability, but also to guard against the gravitational pull of that which is easy and populist. The Aldeburgh Festival never came near to even the edge of that trap, even though it did have years when the money was hard to find.

It was the mix of the presence of two of the most exciting musicians in England with Britten's compositions of locally based music that provided the essential ingredients for what proved to be a lasting, responsive and appreciative Suffolk audience. The Aldeburgh Festival, in English cultural life, is a phenomenal occurrence, unmatched in the country's history. It is Benjamin Britten's greatest invention and legacy. He may, in many ways and for perfectly understandable reasons, have been a difficult person to accept, but, for Aldeburgh, this contribution to the town's heritage has been exceptional.

The initial plan was to hold the festival over a week in June and to use the Jubilee Hall, the cinema, the church and the Baptist Chapel as venues. In the first year there would be three performances of *Albert Herring* and a number of other concerts and talks. The gamble was whether the opera in the Jubilee Hall could have an orchestral performance or whether it would have to be accompanied by pianos. In the event, the orchestra of the English Opera Group was squeezed in 'with very little elbow room', whilst every movement on stage was executed with absolute precision, in order to avoid any unintentional incident.

There has always been more than a sufficient strain of good taste in Suffolk to appreciate such a great artistic gift to the county, and the success of the Aldeburgh Festival was immediate. Britten and Pears' ability to make artistic friendships among their own generation also played its part. Although Peter Pears talked of 'a few friends', he proved that he and Britten were able to draw upon the performances of many of the most remarkable musicians of the post-war era, without limit or political boundary. As a result, for many people the word 'Aldeburgh' has come to mean a week or two in June during which there is a programme of superb musical and cultural events in glorious surroundings.

At an early stage Britten and Pears enlisted sage experience from the Earl of Cranbrook and his wife at nearby Glemham House. There is a touch of the children's party about many of Britten's works, and he delighted in working and making music with young people.

The stained glass memorial window in St Peter and St Paul church was created by John Piper and depicts scenes from three of Britten's church parables: *The Prodigal Son*, *Curlew River*, and *The Burning Fiery Furnace*. It was dedicated to Britten's memory in June 1980. Reproduced by permission of the Piper estate, courtesy of the Britten-Pears Foundation.

The nursery for *The Little Sweep* was modelled on the nineteenth-century home of Margery Spring-Rice at Iken Hall, and the parts of the children in the first production were played by the Cranbrook children and their two cousins, who supplied names for the children in the opera.

Noye's Fludde, Britten's church drama for young people, is the ideal tale for the sea-swept coast and was first performed in the church at Orford. In it the animals preparing for the ark are all children in costume, and the raindrops of the storm are famously invoked by tapping against half-filled glasses of water. This truly was Britten in the element that was closest to Aldeburgh and its country. It is also the perfect way for church buildings to be used, invoking their ancient role as centres of family and community as they were always intended to be used. It was no accident that the Aldeburgh festival made such good use of the local churches as far afield as the stunningly beautiful one at Blythburgh, which is not only a visual delight but also has clear and perfect acoustic properties for music.

The post-war musical festival brought Aldeburgh to the centre of cultural fashion. In the 1950s a new age of stereophonic high fidelity recording of classical works created a market for performers. Britten and Pears, the BBC and recording companies were all the focus of attention and finance, and the next twenty-five years witnessed a golden era for classical music. Each June there gathered in the little seaside town some of the most important international cultural figures of the age.

Noye (Owen Brannigan) receives the olive branch in the first production of Britten's *Noye's Fludde*, June 1958. Photographer Kurt Hutton.
Reproduced courtesy of the Britten-Pears Foundation.

The festival was born of an ideal - enduringly and honourably maintained - which was expressed perfectly by Peter Pears in the introduction to a catalogue of paintings in 1955:

'Of the arts: music, painting, poetry, the one which should absorb our interest more than any other is contemporary art, the work which is being done here and now. The Mirror, the Echo, the Conscience, even the Spectre of today, we cannot deny it. Whether we like it or not, it is the great part of ourselves and to disregard it is to miss an integral experience of our lives. The great work of the past is there, solid, admirable, inevitable, but to attend at the creation of the art of our time, to encourage and to sympathize - and with luck to take part in it - that is the unique and privileged opportunity that comes of being born at a certain time and in a certain place. It is a privilege which I have no intention of foregoing, indeed I shall continue to exercise it as long as I can.'

2008 was the fiftieth anniversary of the premiere of *Noye's Fludde*, and to commemorate the occasion the Jubilee Opera mounted a special performance in Orford church, directed by Frederic Wake-Walker and conducted by Stewart Bedford. Photograph by Dave Herman. Reproduced by kind permission of Jubilee Opera.

By the 1960s Britten was a national figure, and his house on the sea front attracted so much attention that it disturbed him from the work of composition. He and the painter Mary Potter agreed an exchange of local properties, and Britten took up residence in The Red House in a private road alongside the golf course. This became the centre of the lives of the two musicians and now holds Britten's library for the use of students and scholars.

In The Red House, party games seem to have been the order of the day. Mary Potter painted a set of playing cards with which to play Happy Families, a traditional English card game. These portray local people in the town, known to Britten and Pears and their friends, and they still remain in the library of The Red House long after the last players have all departed.

In 1965 Britten approached the management of the Old Maltings at Snape. He wished to develop the largest building of Victorian magnate Newson Garrett's great industrial creation into a concert hall, and the home of the Aldeburgh festival. Britten must have seen the building for years and wandered alongside it when he lived in the old mill. The

View above Snape Maltings, and down the River Alde to the sea. Photograph by Mike Page, reproduced by kind permission of the photographer.

Mary Potter, Playing cards. The artist Mary Potter was a great friend of Benjamin Britten and Peter Pears, and was a regular guest at The Red House each Christmas when they played the card game 'Happy Families'. One Christmas she presented them with a set of cards that she had painted with carefully-observed pictures of local people from Aldeburgh, with their names all changed. The cartoons were witty and not at all cruel, and the present was a big success.

Reproduced with permission of the Potter estate, (DACS), courtesy of the Britten-Pears Foundation.

Jonathan Trim, Low Tide at Snape.
Reproduced by kind permission of the artist.

building was duly completed, however disaster struck a year after it opened, when either by accident of cigarette or iron in the dressing room, the concert hall burned down in a catastrophic fire.

The festival performance was moved that night and took place in the church at Blythburgh. Within a year the entire hall was rebuilt with small improvements learned during the first construction. It is a wonderful hall, striking both from the outside and in, and the sound quality in the concert area is so superior that it is used for recording by the best musicians in the world. It was built less than a hundred years after Garrett's death and his children were still working in the adjacent buildings within the family business. From the glacier-like slate roof to the warm brick foyer, it is a continuous pleasure within its rural environment, of which one feels the gentleman entrepreneur and his daughters would have been so proud. Newson Garrett was a practical man with an architect's eye and has influenced so much that is Aldeburgh and its landscape.

In recent years a second, and smaller concert hall has been added for more intimate and dramatic performances, and today Snape Maltings is the great musical centre of the Britten-Pears legacy, with two concert halls and a music school in adjacent buildings overlooking the estuary. With this vibrant and evolving testimony to their work, there was no need for further public monument in Aldeburgh, but there are several more. There is a fine stained glass window created by John Piper in a north window of the church; two headstones in the Aldeburgh graveyard stand like silent men calling for the ages to weary their marble; and on the beach the Maggi Hambling sculpted seashell carries the inscription 'I hear those voices that will not be drowned' from the libretto of *Peter Grimes*.

Glynn Thomas, Britten's Beach, 2011, etching, 42 x 14cm. Reproduced by kind permission of the artist.

CHAPTER 3:

THE ALDEBURGH FESTIVAL

BRITTEN'S LEGACY

The Aldeburgh Festival – and its associated activities – form one of the most profound achievements in the English arts since the Second World War.

In 1967 the performance centre of the Festival was moved from the town of Aldeburgh. The chosen location was in a newly-built concert hall in the old agricultural maltings buildings at Snape situated at the head of the river Alde and originally designed and built by the Victorian entrepreneur, Newson Garrett.

The largest and finest of these structures became the principle concert venue but at the same time the festival continued to operate in the Jubilee Hall, in Aldeburgh church, the cinema and other buildings in the town. The new building was opened by Her Majesty the Queen who seems to have had a very special relationship with Benjamin Britten and Peter Pears over many years, since Britten wrote *Gloriana* in celebration of her coronation and his own arrangement of the National Anthem.

Thomas Adès, musical director of the festival from 1999-2009 conducting the Aldeburgh Festival orchestra in 2007. Photograph by Malcolm Watson, reproduced by kind permission of the photographer.

Opposite:
Helen Dougall, The Cellist, batik, 2010, 48 x 56cm. Reproduced by kind permission of the artist.

47

Only two years after the grand opening the concert hall was destroyed by fire in June 1969. Photograph by Clive Strutt, reproduced by kind permission of the photographer.

It is hard to conceive of the despair that must have been felt when on an evening during the events of the 1969 festival, the roof of the brand new concert hall caught fire and burned down. After years of striving, fund-raising, planning and that kind of committed belief that is close to fantasy, the dream of a large hall for international performances was destroyed overnight. Cruelty is an understatement for what all those involved must have felt.

Yet the festival that year went on – the operatic performance was moved to the angelic and extraordinary medieval church at Blythburgh and within only two years a new hall was constructed 'learning the lessons from the building of the former one'. There are photographs of Britten on the next morning near to the twisted and smouldering remains of his grand piano which had been on the stage for the performance of the previous evening.

By the time of the fire in 1969, the programme of the festival was populated by some of the most famous and presitigious musicians in the world. The list of composers whose works were performed and the artists who played them is an encyclopaedia of twentieth-century music.

Benjamin Britten and Peter Pears were by turns described as 'difficult', 'odd', 'magical' and many other things – but the heart of their work, and their legacy, is the highest level of sustained musical creation.

The new concert hall gave an extra dimension to the festival as they intended it would. Britten and Pears, together with their close friend Imogen Holst, created unique festival programmes. By 1982 there had been world premieres of fifteen operas. The first performance outside Russia of Shostakovich's Symphony Number 14, of which Britten is the dedicatee, took place in Snape in 1970; Sviatoslav Richter gave a recital in the presence of HRH Queen Elizabeth the Queen Mother. Simon Rattle has conducted many times and the list of outstanding performers has included Janet Baker, Dietrich Fisher-Dieskau, John Shirley-Quirk and a host of other names.

Britten and Pears – and their own personal friends – dominated the festival for its first forty years. After them, while it might all have dwindled, Aldeburgh music found another rich stream of invention that has sustained and developed its scope. Somehow it has avoided turning into a nostalgia for what happened – it is just a much an invention and a challenge as ever it was.

In 1997 Jonathan Reekie became Chief Executive and in 1999 the English composer Thomas Adès was appointed Artistic Director of the Festival, to be followed in 2009 by the French pianist Pierre Laurent-Aimard.

Her Majesty Queen Elizabeth opened the Snape Maltings concert hall in 1967. Photograph by Clive Strutt, reproduced by kind permission of the photographer.

Ros Donaldson, Festival 50, 1998, mixed media, 185 x 145cm. Reproduced by kind permission of the artist.

Why not have an Aldeburgh Festival?

5th June 1948 —
first notes Chacony in G minor
Purcell arranged by BB

Parish Church Aldeburgh

Jubilee Hall

Arnold Holloway
Musgrave Maconchy
Oldham Harrison-Birtwistle Hooddinott Turnage Willcocks
Rostropovich Gross Avonowitz Luxon Norrington Harper Maxwell Knussen Bennett Weir
Vishnevskaya Henze Bedford Horszowski Maw Raitt Finnis Davies Lindberg Dutilleux Norman Armstrong Hyndman Ades Le Fann Shelton Brown Rolfe-Johnson

The Little Sweep

Curlew River

Rape of Lucretia 87

A Midsummers Night's Dream 60

Noye's Fludde Vile

...son Nolan Piper Potter Richards Somerville Vaughan

ARNE ARNOLD
ADES BACH BARTOK
BEETHOVEN BERG
BERKELEY BIRTWISTLE
BRAHMS BRIDGE
BRITTEN BYRD
BRUCKNER BERLIOZ
CAMPION COPLAND
CARTER CHOPIN
DEBUSSY DOWLAND
DUTILLEUX ELGAR
FALLA FAURE FOSS
GERSHWIN GRAINGER
GRIEG HANDEL HAYDN
HENZE HINDEMITH
HOLLOWAY HOLST
IRELAND IVES
JANACEK KIRCHNER
KNUSSEN LISZT
LUTOSLAWSKI MATHENS
MENDELSSOHN MAHLER
MESSIAEN MONTEVERDI
MOZART MUSSORGSKY
NIELSEN POULENC
PROKOFIEV PURCELL
RAKHMANINOV RAVEL
ROSSINI RUDERS SCARLATTI
SCHOENBERG SCHNITTKE
SCHUBERT SCHUMANN
SHOSTAKOVICH SIBELIUS
STRAUSS STRAVINSKY
TAVENER TAVERNER
TELEMANN TIPPETT
TCHAIKOVSKY TURNAGE
VAUGHAN WILLIAMS
VERDI VILLA-LOBOS
VIVALDI WAGNER WALTON
WARLOCK WEBER WOLF

Elizabeth Sweeting 48 - 55
Stephen Reiss 56 - 71
William Servaes 72 - 80
Jack Phipps 81 - 82
Kenneth Baird 83 - 88
Sheila Colvin 89 -

— General Directors —

Following the process of development that originated with Britten and Pears, the musical centre expanded at the same high standard to include events and performances throughout the year. Another set of concerts, initially led by the cellist Mstislav Rostropovich, became known as the 'Aldeburgh Proms' and are now established as a major event in the musical calendar each autumn.

A desire to pass on the founders' musical values led to the Britten Pears Young Artist Programme, Aldeburgh Residencies, the Britten Sinfonia, Faster than Sound, Place, Aldeburgh Young Musicians, Aldeburgh Education – and a host of other platforms for English music. Snape has become an international musical conservatoire crossed with a young and vibrant circus of the outrageous. The possibilities it offers are wonderful. The achievements are thrilling. The form is not just music but many arts and disciplines and the participation is not just the highest grade of musicians, but people from all stages and aspirations: the young, the deprived, the imprisoned, as well as the advantaged and the eager. The arts at Aldeburgh now include events celebrating poetry and the written word, painting, sculpture, photography and dance, and the facilities are used by a variety of local and national organisations.

In 2009 the Britten Studio in the new Hoffman building and the Jerwood 'Kiln Studio' were opened. Both are excellent additions to the available venues for performance. The festival has always used local buildings and places, and there have been performances on Aldeburgh beach, on the sea front at Sizewell power station and at the former American Air Force base at Bentwaters near Woodbridge.

A visitor to Snape, for any of the musical events, finds adventure among the old buildings and the landscape. They are an extraordinary set of constructions, each one of which must have had definite purpose and have been needed, but many now stand bedraggled and in need of repair. One wishes that it were possible to restore each one to its original state and then leave it empty for the excitement it would give. Alongside the reed beds as one walks down to the Alde, these architectural delights are themselves musical. There are pathways, mostly without signs, that lead one to Iken Church, and Snape racecourse and the salt marshes.

The University of Essex choir, with conductor Richard Cooke, one of the many local organisations who have been able to take advantage of the superb facilities at Snape Maltings.

Opposite page: *Netia Jones,* 'Everlasting Light – projections onto Sizewell nuclear power station', May 2012.
Reproduced by kind permission of the artist.
Photograph by Nat Urazmetova.

'Here are the walks of Benjamin Britten', says the Festival programme, but they are also the walks of Saxons, Vikings and Romans and the military of the Second World War – and of the formidable children of Newson Garrett in their formative years. They are also the walks of the contemplative and the bird watchers of the present time.

If the oldest tradition of Aldeburgh is the antagonistic relationship between the fishermen and the burghers, as was clear to the ancient Bishop of Colchester and the Tudor merchants and repeated down the years to the story of Peter Grimes, then in a way the festival has to live with the same fault line. 'How can an Aldeburgh festival be based at Snape?'; 'What happened to the Festival Club?' – which was an expression of upper class patronage that is no longer in existence – and 'Does the Aldeburgh festival belong to the people of the town or does it belong to The Arts Council?' these are all questions that history has proved are impossible to answer. They can't be. Because Aldeburgh is a sea town and not an inland town, it will always have its own independent regime and character. The festival is part of that. It will not conform to acceptable prediction and practice and nor should it. There will always be anxious conflict among the locals, just as there are rainy days on a beautiful landscape. That is part of the frisson and the pleasure that a visitor experiences.

The 2007 production of Britten's *Death in Venice* at Aldeburgh, with Alan Oke as Aschenbach, directed by Yoshi Oida and conducted by Paul Daniel. Photograph by Malcolm Watson, reproduced by kind permission of the photographer.

But it is music that matters and it is enlightening to recount the vast array of talent that has been on show in the past decade alone. Opening a page of the programme at random from 2007 reveals, in one day, performances of the works of Gesualdo, Monteverdi, Salvatore Sciarino, Niccolo Castigione, Giacinto Sclesi and – of course – Benjamin Britten.

Laurie Rudling, Suffolk Coastal, collagraph, 46 x 28cm. Reproduced by kind permission of the artist.

There was a performance of Britten's *Death in Venice* at the Maltings and a showing of Luchino Visconti's film adaptation of the same Thomas Mann story in the Aldeburgh cinema. In the evening Arnold Schoenberg's daughter, Nuria, introduced a work for two violins written by her late husband Luigi Nono in the Jubilee Hall.

Each day of that same festival produced an extraordinary patchwork of contact with the musical world. These things are not just the product of great invention, they also need energy, dedication and hard labour which fill the visitor with admiration and enjoyment.

2013 (the year of publication of this book) marked the 100th anniversary of the birth of Benjamin Britten. The celebrations were to last for more than a year from the date of his birth, 22 November, in 2012, and featured – in the spirit of its very origins – six world first performances especially commissioned for the centenary by the composers Judith Weir, Magnus Lindberg, Poul Ruders, Wolfgang Rihm, Richard Rodney Bennett and Harrison Birtwistle.

There were talks and debates; explorations of the landscape and of the idea that a place could mean so much and have such influence upon international artists and art. It was a busy year for the town, but while much happened, little changed.

CHAPTER 4:

SHAPE, SHADOW AND FORM

THE ART OF ALDEBURGH

In contrast to other towns Aldeburgh has prospered from its eccentricity and its inheritance of genuine culture. If ever a place showed the foolishness of 'dumbing down' and the madness of easy 'heritage' initiatives that have taken place elsewhere, it is not here. The cultural integrity of the numerous festivals held in Aldeburgh each year has allowed the town to grow and hold its head high when the art of much of rural England has declined.

Chrissy Norman, Sculpture in the Reed Beds, etching, 11 x 25cm.
Reproduced by kind permission of the artist.

The Aldeburgh Festival has provided a home for British and international artists and sculptors of several generations and movements since the war. Visitors to Snape Maltings are familiar with the sculptures of Barbara Hepworth and Henry Moore which frame the view over the Alde, and have always seemed so natural and appropriate to the setting. The set designers who have worked on the festival since its origin have also provided a legacy of creation which is peculiar to the Aldeburgh heritage.

The most adventurous approach to Aldeburgh is on foot from the south through Sudbourne and across the river Alde. From here the traveller obtains the best view of the town. Nowadays the route is almost impossibly overgrown but for several hundred years the passenger ferry at Slaughden was operated and this was the way that J.M.W. Turner arrived whilst on a journey through Suffolk in the 1820s. Turner travelled up the coast with his sketch books. He made several pencil sketches and two major paintings, one of Aldeburgh and the other of Orford. At this time Crespigny House, which can be seen in the painting overleaf, was the largest building in the town apart from the church and the Martello Tower which had been constructed about twenty years before.

J.M.W. Turner, Aldborough (sic), Suffolk,
c. 1826, watercolour and gouache
on paper, 28 x 40cm.
Taken from a series of coloured
engravings, 'Picturesque Views of
England and Wales' published by
Charles Heath between 1826 and 1832.
(Tate Gallery)

Thomas Churchyard, Figures and Boats on the Beach,
watercolour, 12 x 20.5cm.
Private collection

John Piper, Beanfield with Church Tower.
Reproduced by permission of the Piper estate,
courtesy of the Britten-Pears Foundation.

J.M.W. Turner, Aldborough (sic), c. 1825-29, watercolour over pencil heightened with bodycolour. Private collection, USA, courtesy of Lowell Libson Ltd, London.

Crabbe's poem *The Borough* had been published in 1816, and the town was much as the poet had seen it, with its struggling fishermen and boatyards on the one hand, but on the other its smart visitors seeking amusements in the summer.

Turner's beautiful painting conveys the interest of arriving at a Georgian seaport and the impression it creates is of the industry and trade that one no longer sees. The Church stands high but there are already large mansions visible in the town. The windmill in the painting can still be seen, as can the Martello Tower – at the time a recent construction – that was a fortress lookout, and a garrison for troops to protect the coastline from Napoleonic invasion.

Left:
Trevor Woods, Barbara Hepworth
Sculpture, Snape, 2009, acrylic and
ink on heavyweight watercolour
paper, 26 x 37cm.
Reproduced by kind permission of
the artist, courtesy of Aldeburgh
Contemporary Arts.

Right:
Tom Cringle, The Lifeboat Station,
acrylic on canvas, 70 x 60cm.
Reproduced by kind permission
of the artist.

Alone on a stretch of the beach stands
'Scallop', the four-metre-high
sculpture by Maggi Hambling. The
largest of the two interlocking shells is
pierced with the words: 'I hear those
voices that will not be drowned', from
the libretto of *Peter Grimes*.
Maggi Hambling, Scallop, 2003,
approx 4m x 4m, corrrugated steel.
Reproduced by kind permission
of the artist.

Jules George, Promenade II, 2008,
oil on linen, 54 x 65cm.
Reproduced by kind permission of the artist.

Jules George, Promenade, 2008,
oil on canvas, 40 x 50cm.
Reproduced by kind permission of the artist.

Jonathan Trim, Towards Aldeburgh on a Bright Morning.
Reproduced by kind permission of the artist.

Jonathan Trim, Low Tide Near Aldeburgh.
Reproduced by kind permission of the artist.

CHAPTER 5:
WRITERS AND THINKERS

Authors of great quality and reputation have written about Aldeburgh or used it as a backdrop for their fictional creations. Many imaginative visitors are inspired by what they find. For others a fascination with the local history and the atmospheric landscape are a source of inspiration.

Of them all, only the native born George Crabbe really describes in detail the brutal reality of his own experience, which is why in spite of the quality and power of his language, he is often not popular with local readers who would prefer a prettier view.

The Aldeburgh of storms, poverty and isolation was the place where George Crabbe grew up. No one has described the town more powerfully or with such brutal honesty. His father was the Collector of Salt Duties and worked in the Old Custom House which still stands at the south end of the High Street. The steps, which are still in their original place, led to the Customs Master's office above, and below was a store for contraband goods and the gaol for smugglers.

Late in his life, George Crabbe described vividly the desperate realities of life by the sea that he witnessed in his childhood:

Right:
George Crabbe's parents' house was on the seafront near the Moot Hall, on one of the streets washed away by flooding in the 1700s. That destruction was the single biggest change in the coastline Aldeburgh has ever seen take place. 'The house in which Crabbe the poet was born', line engraving, nineteenth century, artist unknown.

Opposite:
George Crabbe (1754-1832), line engraving by W. Hull, after a painting by Thomas Philips RA. First published by John Murray, 1860. (Trowbridge Museum)

Moothall Aldeburgh   Glynn Thomas

'The outskirts of the Borough reach,
And these half-buried buildings next the beach,
Where hang at open doors the net and cork,
While squalid sea-dames mend the meshy work;
Till comes the hour when fishing through the tide
The weary husband throws his freight aside;
A living mass which now demands the wife,
Th' alternate labours of their humble life.'

Crabbe not only wrote about the people of the town, but he was also an observant naturalist who captured the damp and muddy landscape in detail:

'With ceaseless motion comes and goes the tide,
Flowing, it fills the channel vast and wide;
Then back to sea, with strong majestic sweep
It rolls, in ebb yet terrible and deep;
Here Samphire-banks and Saltwort bound the flood,
There stakes and sea-weeds withering on the mud;
And higher up, a ridge of all things base,
Which some strong tide has roll'd upon the place'

Yet it is in the sordid political dealings of the borough and its jealous citizens that Crabbe captured the essence of a squalid, undignified, isolated town. His sad tale of the parish clerk who steals from the church collection plate thinking that no one will notice is as powerful a narration of humiliation in a small community as can be found anywhere. The theft is discovered when the parish clerk is forced to turn out his pockets in front of the church committee. Yet his punishment for being found out is only and no more than that everybody in the town knows what he has done:

'He lived in freedom, but he hourly saw
How much more fatal justice is than law
He saw another in his office reign
And his mild master treat him with disdain
He saw that all men shunned him, some reviled
The harsh passed frowning and the simple smiled
The town maintained him but with some reproof
And clerks and scholars proudly kept aloof'

In Crabbe's story the guilty but educated man eventually retires shamefully to his loft in the town 'and expires'.

70

Opposite page: *Glynn Thomas*, Moot Hall, 2011, etching, 13 x 37cm. Reproduced by kind permission of the artist.

Customs House, High Street, photographed by Gary Radford. Reproduced by kind permission of the photographer.

The Edwardian writer Edward FitzGerald worked throughout his life on the text of the mighty Rubaiyyat by the Persian poet Omar Khayyam. A well-known local figure, he lived in Woodbridge, and used to anchor his boat off Aldeburgh beach. FitzGerald made five translations of the Rubaiyyat. In the first edition a paragraph was translated as follows:

Wake! For the Sun who scattered into flight
The stars before him from the Field of Night,
Drives Night along with them from Heaven and strikes
The Sultan's turret with a Shaft of Light

By the fifth edition this translation had evolved into the following evocative scene, familiar to anyone who has watched the sun rise from Crag Path,

'Awake for morning in the bowl of night
Has flung the stone that puts the stars to flight
And Lo! The hunter of the east has caught
The Sultan's Turret in a noose of light'

Strafford House on Crag Path was the meeting place of a group of distinguished writers and artists who termed themselves 'The Rationalists'. Their host was Edward Clodd who had written a short guide to the town in 1861. Clodd's home, which still stands in the centre of the promenade, was decorated by the architect Charles Voysey. Each Whitsuntide, in the manner of Victorian gentleman's clubs, Edward Clodd invited this group to stay. They included Thomas Hardy, J. M. Barrie (who wrote *Peter Pan* and publicized the development of Thorpeness), George Meredith, George Gissing, Holman Hunt and H. G. Wells.

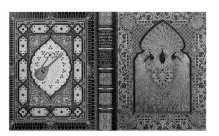

The opulent 'Great Omar' binding of the *Rubaiyyat of Omar Khayyam* contained over a thousand precious and semi precious stones and over one hundred square feet of gold leaf. It was created over two and a half years by the craftsmen at the Sangorski and Sutcliffe bindery in London, and finally completed in 1911. Sent to America on the *Titanic*, it perished when the ship sank. (Courtesy Shepherd's Bindery)

Clodd made his money in banking but had published several books on the work of Charles Darwin. He also suggested that any events or descriptions in the Bible could be explained by the theory of evolution. H. G. Wells rather ungenerously described his host as a 'customs officer at pains to banish God from the universe'. Nevertheless, Clodd was an important figure in Aldeburgh life, and an expert on the history of the town. His book about Aldeburgh was revised and republished by his son and is an important source of reference.

'The Place on the Map' (Thomas Hardy)

I
'I look upon the map that hangs by me —
Its shires and towns and rivers lined in varnished artistry —
And I mark a jutting height
Coloured purple, with a margin of blue sea.

II
—'Twas a day of latter summer, hot and dry;
Ay, even the waves seemed drying as we walked on, she and I,
By this spot where, calmly quite,
She informed me what would happen by and by.

III
This hanging map depicts the coast and place,
And re-creates therewith our unexpected troublous case
All distinctly to my sight,
And her tension, and the aspect of her face.

IV
Weeks and weeks we had loved beneath that blazing blue,
Which had lost the art of raining, as her eyes of late had too,
While she told what, as by sleight,
Shot our firmament with rays of ruddy hue.

V
For the wonder and the wormwood of the whole
Was that what in realms of reason would have joyed our double soul
Wore a torrid tragic light
Under order-keepings rigorous control.

VI
So, the map revives her words, the spot, the time,
And the thing we found we had to face before the next year's prime;
The charted coast stares bright,
And its episode comes back in pantomime.'

Michelle Holmes, 'The Fisherman Brings in his Catch', 2012. Cyanotype. Machine, hand stitching and applique, on cotton, linen and velvet, 55 x 53cm. Photograph by Terry Davies, artwork reproduced by kind permission of the artist.

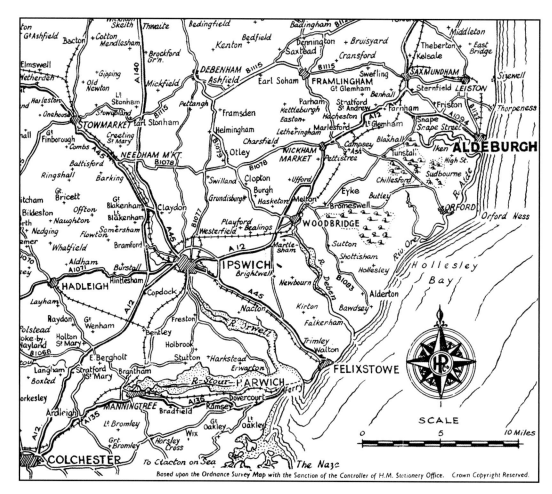

A map of Aldeburgh and the vicinity. The branch railway line between Aldeburgh, Leiston and Saxmundham can be seen, although this stretch of line has long since closed.
Map based on 1958 Ordnance Survey map, reproduced with permission of the Ordnance Survey.

The Rationalists were all declared atheists. Their central thesis was that science is rational and the idea of a God is therefore irrational because there is no scientific evidence for his or her existence. Karl Marx and later Bertrand Russell also followed the same line and believed that religion had been used to brainwash people ('Religion is the opiate of the masses') and to stop them thinking rationally. George Meredith said 'A man who has no mind of his own lends it to the priests'.

Of this group of famous authors and artists who were acquainted with Edward Clodd, George Gissing is the dark horse. His melancholy tales of failure as an author and attempts at describing his own unhappy relationships belong to another time and he is closer to the Aldeburgh of George Crabbe than his fellow would-be philosophers. It is hard even to picture him at the same supper table as the others. Twice he married prostitutes, and he even went to prison for stealing for one of them. His book *The New Grub Street* is a remarkable and funny tale of failure and the squalour it brings.

Wilkie Collins' book *No Name* is set in Aldeburgh and contains vivid descriptions of the 'Parade' along 'the sea front', as he calls it, in thinly disguised fiction. He had told his mother that he would break his journey from York with a short holiday in Lowestoft but it appears from the book that he came to Aldeburgh instead, and was much taken with all he found on Crag Path. As Captain Wragge, a character in the book says 'There is only one walk in the place...and on that walk we must all meet every time we go out.'

Magdalen, the heroine, decides that, deprived of her fortune and her true love, and forced to marry the evil Noel Vanstone, she will kill herself with an overdose of

74

'On What Chance', an illustration of the heroine Magdalen, counting ships from her window at North Shingles Villa, Aldeburgh, a bottle of poison on the windowsill. 'For one half hour to come, she determined to wait there and count the vessels as they went by. If in that time an even number passed her – the sign given, should be a sign to live. If the uneven number prevailed – the end should be Death.' Engraving by John Everett Millais from *No Name*, by Wilkie Collins, 1863.

laudanum. The final decision to proceed depends upon the number of ships that pass on the horizon in thirty minutes as she watches from a hotel bedroom window. If there is an even number she will live, but if the number is odd she will take the laudanum and lay against the window ledge to accept her fate.

Wilkie Collins appears to have stayed only a few days in the town in 1861, just after his novel *The Woman in White* had become a bestseller. *No Name* was published in serial format in 1862 and the illustrations by Millais were published in the bound edition of the book published in 1864.

At the same time as Clodd and his friends were pursuing their their anti-religious intellectual debates in a fine house on the sea front, the vicar of Aldeburgh was equally hard at work trying to care for his parishioners. After Robert Topcliffe of the Puritan era, the most famous vicar the town has had is Henry Thompson, who ministered at the church from 1874. The details of his life in the parish are known because of the book about him written by his daughter, Dorothy. She called him 'Sophia's Son', and her tales of the town are far more illuminating than the sometimes ponderous verses of the Rationalists.

Dorothy Thompson and her father, Reverend Henry Thompson, vicar of Aldeburgh from 1874-1904. (From *Sophia's Son* by Dorothy Thompson, Terence Dalton Publishing, Lavenham, 1969)

The architect, poet and painter Cecil Lay (1885-1956) lived in Aldringham next to Aldeburgh for most of his life.

Reverend Thompson was employed by Leveson Vernon Wentworth and lived within the compass of the famous Garrett family across the road. He was responsible not only for the parish in Aldeburgh, but also that of Blackheath, which was part of the Wentworth estate. The Wentworths built a new vicarage close to the church for Henry Thompson and his family. Unfortunately it is no longer standing, which would be no surprise to Dorothy who recorded its failings and shortcomings as a child. She said it was dark, damp and drafty. Although the book is properly about her father, the heroine of most of the stories she tells is her mother Georgina Thompson.

A very different kind of literary fame for Aldeburgh came from the children's character Orlando the Marmalade Cat. In 1938 the first of the Orlando stories was published by Country Life Ltd., with text and illustrations by Kathleen Hale. In the 1952 story of 'A Seaside Holiday', Orlando takes his family to 'Owl Barrow' which is clearly recognisable as Aldeburgh, where they stay in a large house boat on the beach.

The boat in the Orlando stories was real and was called *Ionia*, and it stood for many years beached on the mudflats near the boatyard at Slaughden. During the First World War, it was a home for young girls who were refugees from Belgium and no doubt a few river animals as well, grateful for warmth and food.

It is not just in Aldeburgh and Snape that creative art has flourished. Cecil H. Lay was a poet and architect with a house in Aldringham called 'Raidsend' which he designed and built just before the Great War. A visitor to Mr Lay's house said he found 'a tall elderly man talking to a white goose. He was dressed in very pale faded Edwardian tweeds and a white silk scarf and on his head was one of those round tweed hats that river fishermen wear. His eyes were clear dark grey. His voice belonged to a past far more remote than the Romans or the Saxons.'

Ionia the house boat in 1952, moored on the beach at Slaughden.
(Francis Frith Collection)

By the 1970s *Ionia* had collapsed
and was in a derelict state. It was
ceremonially burnt in 1975.

One is not surprised to read that Lay was caught talking to a goose. Many of his poems are composed around simple discussions with birds and the animals in his garden:

> 'What do you read? I asked the cow
> I read the words upon the sky, was her reply
> What do you sing? I asked, and how?
> I do not sing I do not try
> And why should I when there are skylarks in the sky.'

His poems convey his simple enchantment at the world around him in Suffolk:

> 'My eyes are filled with wonder
> At any little bird
> On every tree and bush I see
> A wing to give an ecstasy
>
> A goldfinch sitting on a thorn
> Can make of me a man reborn
> But sparrows in the mud suffice
> To carry me to Paradise'

He wrote a poem called 'Philosophies', which says:

> 'Philosophies of long ago
> Boiled down to this: 'we do not know'
>
> Disputed questions raised today
> Are answered not by Aye or Nay
>
> Turn not your ear to clever men
> But listen to the lark and wren
>
> Celestial sages blessed their wings
> True wisdom never talks but sings'

Lay also created paintings of local beaches and other scenes, depicting innocence and happiness in a way one envies. After travelling widely during his student days, he came home to the area and remained there for the rest of his life. One of his most beautiful poems explains how it was impossible for him to leave, and it ends with these two lines:

> 'Here I stay and years go by
> And Suffolk knows the reason why.'

Kathleen Hale, A Seaside Holiday. The internationally famous series of children's books about Orlando the Marmalade Cat included a depiction of Aldeburgh or 'Owl Barrow' where Orlando and his family take a holiday in a house boat, clearly modelled on *Ionia*. Orlando and his family have a wonderful time, the holiday culminating in Orlando taking charge of the 'Owl Barrow' lifeboat to rescue a stricken ship.
Reproduced by permission of the estate of Kathleen Hale and Frederick Warne/Penguin Books.

Cecil Lay (1885-1956),
Aldeburgh Beach, 1931,
watercolour.

CHAPTER 6:
EARLY HISTORY

An archaeologists' map in the Moot Hall museum shows how the Romans found Aldeburgh when they worked their way up the coast two thousand years ago in 43 AD. The map shows where the coastline has changed, as it continues to do today. The long straight deposit of shingle where there is now the Martello Tower, Slaughden Quay and boatyard, and all the land which is known as Sudbourne beach and Orford Ness did not then exist. The river Alde flowed straight into the sea. The invaders established camps in Woodbridge, Orford, Snape, Aldeburgh and Dunwich. East Anglia became one of the most developed areas in Roman Britain with the best prepared defensive network, not least because the army anticipated an uprising among the Icene, the people who lived in northern East Anglia. They were also concerned about possible invasions by sea of Saxons and Angles from northern Germany, and Vikings and Norsemen from Scandinavia. The main military Roman road was from Colchester through Saxmundham to Great Yarmouth. This provided communication along the coast but there was also a road from Orford leading directly to Aldeburgh with a sunken causeway across the Alde at Barber's Point. As well as the road network, for which the Romans are famous, they also made use of the sea and the rivers as alternative means of transporting provisions and troops with speed and efficiency.

The coastline in Roman times had many more bays and inlets than it does nowadays. Local people still refer to Sole Bay and Hollesley Bay and other features which are no longer there. However most of the landscape seen by the Romans still remains. Aldeburgh itself was an inhabited hill surrounded on three sides by a large beach. The Roman map shows, too, that in earlier times the flat land below the cliff extended much further east into the sea. It also reveals that there was a port or sea harbour to the north of the town. This harbour became known as the Haven, and played an important role in the history of the town until only a hundred years ago. Nowadays the church and a water tower stand on the hill, together with some prominent houses and a tennis court, but it was always the hill that defined Aldeburgh as a fort: a defendable sea base from which one could watch for aggressive marauders both inland and out into the German ocean; a naval look out. 'Alde – burgh' means 'old – fort' or 'former fortress'. It has carried the name for thousands of years. If the Romans, or the fisherman who kept the fort before them, had a watch tower, the logical place for it must have been on the high ground somewhere near where the church now stands, or along Park Road.

What we call the North Sea was dry land until about 6,000 BC. With no major rivers to cross, it was possible to travel by land from Aldeburgh to Holland. Gradually, over the millennia, the estuary of the Ouse to the north became joined to the estuary of The

Opposite page:
Heather Hodgson, Aldeburgh Marshes, mixed media on canvas, 60 x 51cm. Reproduced by kind permission of the artist.

Overleaf:
Laurence Edwards, Creek Men. Created in 2007 for the 2008 Aldeburgh Festival, these eight-feet-tall primeval figures were first made in clay and then cast in bronze, before being towed through the reed beds overlooking Snape Maltings. Reproduced by kind permission of the artist.

Thames to the south, and the flow of water became a river, which in its turn formed the coast of East Anglia. At some time around then the English Channel opened up as a result of a great flood, and the action of the sea levels rising higher than the land continues in modern times. The amber which is washed up on the beach after a storm is the fossilized sap of ancient trees which stood in forests to the east of the current coastline. The sea defences we use today as pathways along the banks of the Alde, and which temporarily hold back the inexorable progress of the sea over the land, were developed much later in around 1000-1200 AD and have helped to form the current geography of the town and its surrounding landscape.

Halima Washington Dixon, Resonance, 2012, oil on board, 25.5 x 30cm. Reproduced by kind permission of the artist.

A reconstruction of Roman salt working activity in the Aldeburgh area. Artwork by David Gillingwater of Herring Bone Design, reproduced by kind permission of the artist.

The Romans extracted salt from the marshes as far as Snape; it was an essential for an army on the move in order to preserve meat and fish for the soldiers, so salt flats were a desirable military objective. They probably made pottery and bricks from the clay and iron in the red soil. They had a dockyard on the river at Barber's Point, which lies to the south west of the fort and is close to jetties used by more recent brickworks. In peacetime the town thrived. Homes were built on the beach far to the east of the cliff. Invaders from Denmark, Holland and Flanders could be seen approaching and were kept out by strong fishermen who traded their catches for crops and meat from inland merchants. The Roman town of Aldeburgh had more people than Gypswicke (Ipswich) but less than Dunwich to the north which was a larger port.

There are fewer annals or chronicles of East Anglia of the early medieval period, than there are of Ireland, but it is not hard to imagine that this was a settled and prosperous sea-faring settlement. Only an inability to fish would have caused hunger; a plague or a storm at high tide could have done damage, but there was no reason for the whole town to be marooned. As long as a family could move themselves to dry land in a storm, damage to their wooden homes on the beach could be repaired, and there was plenty of wood in the forests inland. Judging from the map, the sea was less likely to cause serious flooding than it might do nowadays, and even then the high ground was easily accessible and must have been well used and populated.

The scarcity of written source material from this part of the world does not mean there were no fishermen's tales, or music, or culture that passed down through the oral tradition. There probably were many stories of storms and sea monsters among

the boatmen and for certain the sea shanties used to give rhythm to the strokes of the oars will have been sung and re-sung in the town. Nor is it hard to believe that the same families whose names appear in the first surviving written records in the 1500s and are still in the town now, were around then and even long before the Romans came. The local family names of Cable, Burwood, Bence, Strowger, Johnson and Ward may have been said slightly differently as accent, dialect and inflection changed, but the essence and the inherited personality must have been much the

Colin Slee, Hazelwood Marshes, 2012, acrylic on paper, 42 x 33cm. Reproduced by kind permission of the artist.

same as it is now. These people did not suddenly form themselves into family units when records began, they have been living and working here a lot longer. Their trades were fishing and boat building, but they would have had religious leaders, teachers, and those with whom they did business. They would have had moral tales of their ancestors and adventures as fascinating as ours: the shame is that any written sources have long since been destroyed.

The residents of Aldeburgh had many opportunities to meet and mix with people in other fishing towns and the people were probably much closer to other seafaring communities than to inland people whom they have always regarded as foreign. They certainly travelled to other European countries: Iceland, Scotland, Denmark, Holland and Flanders and maybe further away. Their fishing trips were long journeys from the earliest times; the men of the town stayed away at sea for many months on their travels.

There were once several streets of houses parallel to those now standing along the sea shore and these were present for hundreds, maybe thousands, of years before storms eventually washed them away and straightened the coast line. What remained of them then are shown on Tudor maps and drawings and they had obviously been established a long time even then. The town had rows of dwellings on the beach in the centre of which a public space was formed. That, in time, became a market-place where the Moot Hall was eventually built in about 1520. 'Moot' means a place for meetings. Most houses in the town were within a few feet of where a boat could be pulled up high out of the water.

Before their army settled and built its towns, roads and defences, the Roman invaders faced a ferocious counter-attack in East Anglia which began in 61AD. Boudica, Queen of the Icene rose up with a huge army to drive out the garrison established at Colchester. There were several contributing factors to this act, but the trigger was the Roman army's treatment of the Icene following the death of King Pratsutagus, husband of Queen Boudica. Icene settlements were plundered, Boudica was flogged, her daughters raped, and many of her tribe suffered equally appalling treatment. From her royal base at Thetford in Norfolk, Boudica gathered her army and moved south. She drove the Romans out of Aldeburgh, back over the River Alde away from Iken and Orford. Iken, named after the Icene, stands on the south bank of the Alde estuary and a mile to the east of it is Yarn Hill. Yarn Hill has never been excavated but it is in the centre of the land where the battle took place. It is an odd, dark, circular mound with dense woodland over it.

The legend of Yarn Hill only exists in local folklore. Although ancient remnants of civilization have been found in the undergrowth of the trees, the story is that the hill may well be a burial ground for a defeated legion, or the resting remains of an English army. It may even be the position from which Boudica consolidated her newly-conquered territory, or alternatively a Saxon palace from a later date built on earlier foundations. It lies directly over the river from the Roman villa that has been discovered at Barber's

Point and could be the southern end of a causeway. The line south of the Alde which passes through Iken and so Yarn Hill may well have been a place for Boudica's army to defend. Support for her army came from both land and sea. These descriptions of the 120,000-strong local uprising come from the Romans' own accounts and they must have been unpleasant to read when they arrived back in Rome.

This is the Roman historian Tacitus' report of the speech made by Queen Boudica in her moment of victory:

> From the pride and arrogance of the Romans nothing is sacred; all are subject to violation; the old endure the scourge, and the virgins are deflowered. But the vindictive gods are now at hand. A Roman legion dared to face the warlike Britons: with their lives they paid for their rashness; those who survived the carnage of that day lie poorly hid behind their entrenchments, meditating nothing but how to save themselves by an ignominious flight. From the din of preparation, and the shouts of the British army, the Romans, even now, shrink back with terror.
> (*The Annals of Tacitus,* Book XIV, translation by Church and Brodribb)

The Icene went forward to force the Romans out of Colchester and then to sack the new settlement at London. Roman historian Cassius Dio recorded that that by the point of their final battle with the Romans, the army of Britons was 250,000-strong – comparable to the current numbers of 138,000 regular and territorial, and 95,800 reserves in the British Army. Such major military progress requires sophisticated administration.

Humiliated, the Romans regrouped at London under the new leadership of Suetonius Paulinus. This time, they drove Boudica and her troops back towards the north west and defeated her somewhere in central England on a battlefield whose location is not known.

Charles Gogin (1844-1931), Boadicea, oil on panel, 36.8 x 63.5cm. (Williamson Art Gallery and Museum, Birkenhead)

Cyndi Speer, Garnet and Gold
(Sutton Hoo), 2011, oils, 100 x 70cm.
Reproduced by kind permission
of the artist.

Tacitus reported with some satisfaction that 80,000 Britons died and that Boudica drank poison. After these violent beginnings, the invading legions began to settle and administer the conquered country. In these circumstances it seems highly logical that Aldeburgh was a Roman fortress: when they re-took the town, the commanding officers must have realised its tactical importance in the defence of the region. They would tolerate no more uprisings in East Anglia and no repeats of the horrific events of Boudica's revolt.

In addition to access by sea, the Romans established three roads to the fort town: one from the north through Leiston to the Haven, one from from Saxmundham in the west, and the third is the road up through Sudbourne and across the river Alde.

The pathways through Sudbourne and on both sides of the river are wild, and the marshlands are enclosed by strong and ancient dykes, now overgrown and used as paths. These were built after the Romans had left in order to reclaim land from the river and from the sea and turn it into fertile grazing.

For several centuries the Romans worked with local people to develop the area. They fathered children and built up a prosprous living by panning salt from the marshlands. Eventually in around 410 AD the Roman occupation ended, and their leaders left. By that time Christianity had become the predominant religion in Western Europe. Religious establishments such as York, Durham and Lindisfarne also became centres of education and culture.

Without the protection of a Roman army the eastern coastline of England became the target of persistent and destructive attack from several directions. This is why many Mediterranean and Middle Eastern countries have many intact remains of the architecture of the Roman Empire, yet England has almost none. We have come to assume that a Roman villa will only be found under a field, but there is a reason for this and it is a sad trail of destruction carried out by successive invaders over several hundred years.

There is nothing left of the Roman villa at Barber's Point or any other construction and almost no remnant of earlier years, unless it is deeply buried and yet to be discovered.

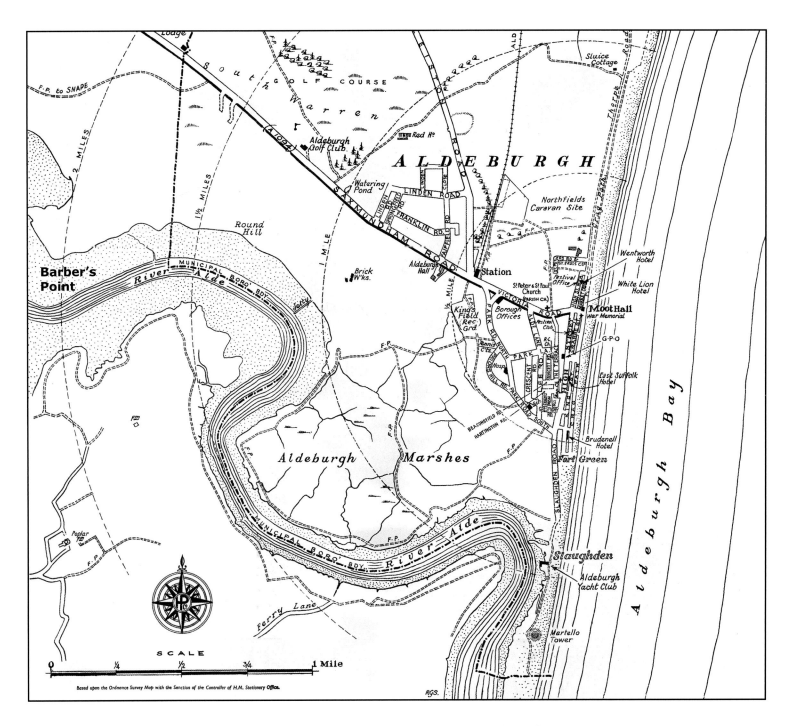

A 1958 map of Aldeburgh and the surrounding area, showing the location of the Roman settlement at Barber's Point (to the west of the town). Excavations in 2004, 2006 and 2010 revealed evidence of an Anglo-Saxon settlement with an early Christian church, as well as large quantities of Roman pottery.

Eventually, though, after years and years of these landings, Saxons also brought prosperity and we know now of several burial areas of important and wealthy figures. Sutton Hoo outside Woodbridge is a striking silent mark on the landscape that leaves one looking at other mounds with curiosity. At Snape there is also a substantial Saxon burial ground which was uncovered during Victorian times.

There is a little signpost on the main road from the A12 to Aldeburgh just after the Snape crossroads that merely says 'By-road' to the right. At this turning, unmarked, in trees, lies an extensive whole Saxon cemetery that was uncovered by Septimus Davidson, a local landowner, in 1862. His excavation revealed evidence of wealth and all the signs of a formal, organised, reverential and hierarchical society, who made their living on the river and at sea as people do now. This part of Snape has been more populous at several times in the past than it is now.

The now-famous burial at Sutton Hoo is said to have taken place in 620 AD, and the one at Snape at about the same time. What has been found in these cemeteries denotes evidence of high craftsmanship and an appreciation of fine artefacts, combined with a dignified respect for the dead.

Burials at this Sutton Hoo site appear to have taken place over about eighty years and ended with the internment of Raedwald, Saxon king of the Wuffings of East Anglia. It is his boat burial that has proved one of the most remarkable archaelogical discoveries. The site overlooks the Deben estuary, which was one of the main Saxon landing sites during the years of their arrival in East Anglia.

Iken church and abbey were founded by Boltolph. The Anglo Saxon Chronicle records that Botolph founded a religious community at Icanho (which means Ox-hill) and that he was buried there. Later his remains were moved to another Burgh near Woodbridge and thence to the church of Bury St Edmunds.

Not only was a church and community built at Iken but there was also a first church built in Aldeburgh around the same time. Architectural studies of the existing Aldeburgh church of St Peter and St Paul show that there was originally a Saxon building on the same site which carried a much lower thatched roof than the current structure. Furthermore, if a Saxon church was built on high ground commanding a view of the marsh and the sea at Iken, then the same logic would have placed one at the lookout position in Aldeburgh. The strategically important points along the coast were those that looked out to the sea and positions commanding the first bridgeable point of a river above its estuary. The view to Aldeburgh church tower from Iken is clear and both could have acted as beacons.

The Anglo Saxon king Raedwald also developed trading links with German and other Mediterranean countries, and Ipswich and its docks prospered under his rule. Raedwald's centre of activity was in Suffolk in the area of the Alde, Deben and Orwell rivers. That is why M. R. James, the nineteenth-century academic and writer of mysteries, drew his conclusions that there must have been a palatial Saxon residence in the area. It seems quite probable that the time around 500-700 AD marks a pause in the perpetual hostilities of the beach and the estuary and the beginning of the development of the town of Aldeburgh we see today.

The Saxons began to organize agriculture and grazing in the lush pastures of Suffolk. Random growths of herbs and greens became fields of corn and barley. Individually-owned cows and sheep became flocks herded for the community. Christianity became dominant in the education and the administration of large parts of the country, and churches were built, mostly in wood, but some in stone, and religious clerics started to write and copy the chronicles of the preceeding centuries. The Anglo Saxon Chronicle and the writings of Augustine, Gildas and Bede still survive from that time.

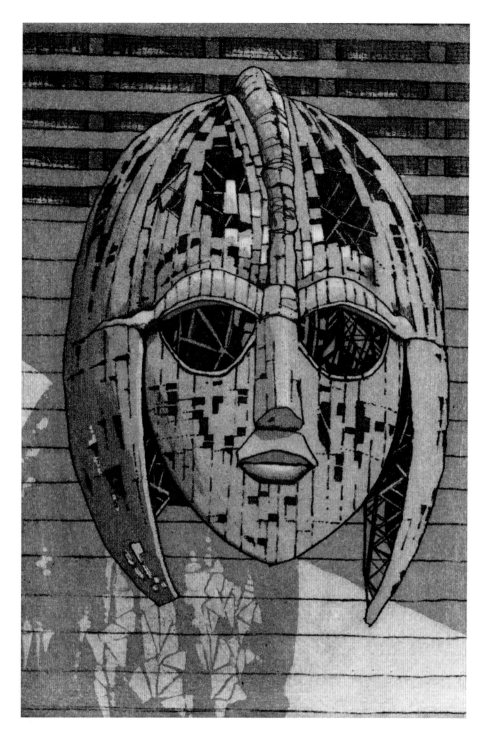

However this peace and prosperity did not last. The new centres of administration and learning attracted a further wave of seaborne invaders. This time it was the Vikings who attacked the east coast in strength, beginning in the north of England at Lindisfarne in 793. Aldeburgh, the Alde and East Anglia soon became a target once again. Like the Saxons before them, the Danish invaders came in pursuit of looting and desecration, and their raids escalated throughout Britain and Ireland. In 865 a large army of Viking Norsemen attacked East Anglia and landed with no opposition. They were led by King Ivar the Boneless and King Halfdan. Having consolidated their hold in East Anglia, they took horses, food and men from the country and moved northward by land whilst their raiding ships moved progressively up the coast. They attacked and took possession of Nottingham, York, Whitby and the Humber, followed by Northumbria. For the many years the Vikings were invincible.

Chrissy Norman, The Helmet, Sutton Hoo, etching, 10 x 15cm. Reproduced by kind permission of the artist.

For the people of Aldeburgh this meant their town was annihilated once again. Anything of worth, any sense of civilization, religious values, culture or community that might have been created by King Raedwald was totally destroyed. Many of the Saxon graves at Snape and at Sutton Hoo and elsewhere were robbed. It is no wonder that so little can be found of Roman, Saxon or prehistoric remains. The town was overrun so often that the people had nowhere to hide or escape, and even fleeing by boat was of no use, as the invading force was a navy with invincible maritime strength.

For two hundred years the Danes continued to invade and fight. The list of battles and campaigns is long and bloody. Contemporary sources recount that King Alfred the Great and his sons and nephews defended the country nobly and courageously, but Alfred did not operate in East Anglia, he was in Wessex. On the coastline of what is now Suffolk, there can never have been a year without troop landings, plunder and preparations for long marches or naval campaigns. There was no peace or stability in East Anglia until the arrival of the French Norman army under William the Conqueror in 1066. Even after the arrival of William's army, East Anglia remained under the rule of the Danish kings to whom William paid large sums that are commonly referred to as Danegeld. These bribes were intended to pay off the Vikings, but their only effect was to make the invaders come back for more. Danegeld has become a word associated with appeasement, and it was a disastrous policy for the kings of England and France as they tried to safeguard their kingdoms. The Domesday Book was prepared by agents of William the Conqueror to describe to him the assets of his conquest. It lists Saxon churches at Aldeburgh, Snape and also at Hazelwood on the north shore of the Alde.

Because the Danes destroyed the Saxon church in Aldeburgh, we have no record of its appearance, but it is likely that it had a round flint tower. The local flint was used as building material because the cut stones are weatherproof and strong. The Saxons built many flint towers in Suffolk and they are circular because the engineering of a circular flint tower is easier and more secure than a square one. It will last longer and hold a stronger platform, and once the foundation is solid it is easier to build a round tower than one with corners that need to be controlled as the building rises. Flint was mined in abundance in Norfolk, near Thetford.

Whatever building work was going on inland during the early years of the Norman invasion, the constant movement of the waves against the shore was also changing the shape of Aldeburgh. It is not known when the shingle banks shifted across the outlet of the Alde to the sea, but during the thousand years from the time of the Roman invasion to 1250 AD, the whole of the estuary closed up and the river entrance diverted south to Orford. The location of the main port of Aldeburgh shifted to what was known as the Haven on the north side of the town, where there is now marshland and cattle grazing to the west of the new road to Thorpeness. All that remains of that bay is the Mere in Thorpeness, but up to the fourteenth century it was a place for unloading coal and loading wool ships. It was the estuary of the river Hundred and provided a refuge to boats coming south down the coast. The Haven had two routes of access: the first from what is now the market square in front of the White Lion Hotel, and the second along Crag Lane which is now an unmade road running from the Leiston Road to a piece of high ground overlooking the sea. This second road features in the M.R. James story of the ancient Saxon burial place of the 'third crown' of England.

The classic ghost story 'A Warning to the Curious' by M.R. James was first published in 1925 and is set in the fictional town of 'Seaburgh', a barely-disguised Aldeburgh. The narrator discovers that three ancient Anglian crowns were buried just outside the town, the last one still guarded by generations of men from a local family. Its resting place is indicated by 'a belt of old firs, wind-beaten, thick at the top'. Peter Polaine, Suffolk Firs, woodcut print, 12.4 x 31.6cm. Reproduced by kind permission of the artist.

CHAPTER 7:
TUDORS

The ascendancy of Henry VII (Henry Tudor) to the throne of England in 1485 was a turning point in the history of the country. For Aldeburgh the impact was huge and at the outset it was about ships. Henry's advisers told him, in simple terms, that the country needed a navy and for that they required more ships. In order to have ships they had to have boat builders who had the administrative support to be ambitious and the financial strength to take risks.

King Henry was prepared to invest in shipbuilding. For him that did not mean giving them money or building dockyards, it meant improving the living boatmen made from what they did every day. His idea was simple: he made the whole country buy fish. He said that English people must eat fish on three days a week. On every day in Lent and during advent and on holy days they must also eat fish. 'Then our boat men and boat-builders will prosper', he said; and they did. The laws were not universally obeyed but they made a difference. The English were required by law to eat fish on more than half the days in the year.

Henry Tudor's reign coincided with the invention of printing in Europe. This ground-breaking leap forward in mass communication not only changed the means of disseminating contemporary thought, but it also changed the language used to express even the simplest ideas. The technology of movable type used to create the first printed books was at least as revolutionary as the invention of radio, television, or the internet in the twentieth century. Henry's advisers now had the means to mould the beginning of an organized legal and fiscal state structure that had sufficient strength to survive the political upheavals of the next two hundred years, and through diligence, discipline and hard work he made England into one of the leading European nations.

This period was an intellectual and artistic era of achievement, the like of which Europe has rarely seen. In Italy, Michelangelo Buonarotti and Leonardo da Vinci created amazing reflections of the world they knew. Vasco da Gama and Christopher Columbus sailed the globe. The books of Erasmus Desideratus from Holland were printed and distributed to of students of philosophy all over Christendom. The weavers of Flanders made tapestries out of dyed english wool at which we still marvel. There was music and philosophy, writing and wit; the universities of Germany and those of Oxford and Cambridge flourished as centres of thought and argument. Artists found expression through their architecture, sculpture, fashion and design in forms dramatically different to any that had gone before. It was an extraordinary time, and opportunities for the brave increased when Henry VlII became King in 1509. For the first twenty years of his reign he added an extra dimension of excitement and learning to the serious legislative work of his father.

Derek Chambers, Moot Hall, etching, 32 x 29cm.
Reproduced by kind permission of the artist, courtesy Aldeburgh Contemporary Art.

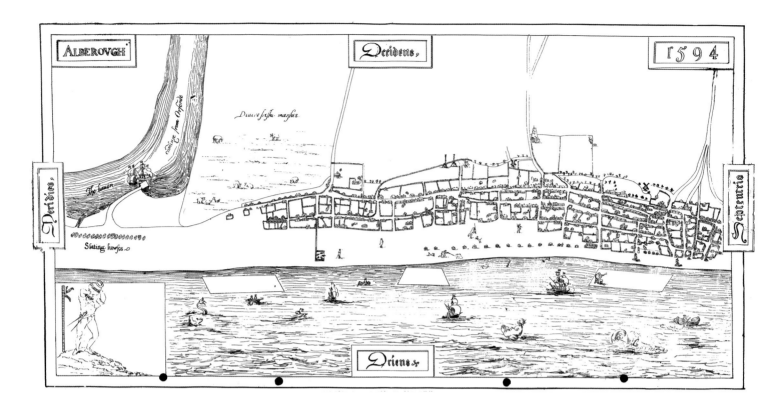

ALBEROVGH   Occidens,   1594

A Tudor map of Aldeburgh, line engraving, 1594. (Ipswich Record Office)

The map of Aldeburgh prepared in 1520 shows the market square with four streets to the east on what is now the beach. There was shipping both on the coast and at Slaughden dock.

Aldeburgh's connection to the major affairs of the Tudor state came directly through the influence of Thomas Wolsey of Ipswich. English school history lessons often present a caricature of Cardinal Wolsey which understates the achievements and misrepresents the motives of one of the most important sons of Suffolk. The Moot Hall and most of the structure of the Church come directly from Wolsey's connection with the town.

If one sees Wolsey from the perspective of his architectural ambition and in the light of his connection to Rome and the Renaissance, he must be regarded as a great creator of Tudor England. In the construction of major Tudor buildings alone, Wolsey commissioned and built the Palace of Whitehall (now the centre of English government); Hampton Court Palace; Christ Church College, Oxford and King's College, Cambridge.

Wolsey briefly held the manor of Aldeburgh and Snape, but his influence on the whole of Suffolk was considerable. In Aldeburgh he must have been regarded as a hero, as he commissioned much of the naval shipbuilding which eventually led to its status as a Borough. Both the Haven, at the north end of the Market Square, and the sheltered dock in the River Alde at Slaughden became important shipping centres.

In the sixteenth century Suffolk was more important in the economy of England than it has been at almost any other time. The revenues from the wool trade together with the strategic importance of its location on the east coast made it a front-line military area, and it was natural that prime agricultural land and the development of domestic and military seafaring should raise its level of importance. Aldeburgh thrived as a working town as never before or since.

Cloth of Gold do not thou dispys
Though thou be mached with Cloth of fries.

Cloth of friez be not thou to bould
Though thou be mached with Cloth of Gold.

Trotter Sculp

Charles Brandon Duke of Suffolk, & Mary Queen of France.

From the Original in the Possession of Sam.ᵗ Egerton Brydges, of Denton in Kent Esq.ʳ

The other local hero at that time was Charles Brandon, Duke of Suffolk (c.1484-1545). Brandon was something of a James Bond figure, who fought and schemed alongside the King and eloped with Henry VIII's younger sister Mary. His dashing, wild, life and his marriage brought pageant, esteem and nobility to the county to the benefit of the whole area.

Charles Brandon and his wife Mary, daughter of Henry VII and sister of Henry VIII. Line engraving by George Vertue after unknown artist, 35.2 x 43.5cm. (National Portrait Gallery)

Charles Brandon, Duke of Suffolk and Mary Tudor were the most glamorous couple of their age. She was married briefly at her brother Henry VIII's insistence, to the elderly French King Louis XII, but the old French monarch died and Suffolk married her before Henry and Wolsey could contrive another arranged wedding for their own diplomatic purposes. Henry was angry with Brandon but he adored his beautiful sister and relented and forgave them. Suffolk became a powerful and close friend of the King. Brandon and Mary married secretly in March 1515 in France but had a second open wedding ceremony in Greenwich in May of the same year, followed by celebrations in Suffolk which brought the whole court to the county.

Nearer to Aldeburgh, the dockyard at Slaughden prospered from about 1490 when it was commissioned to build ships for the defence of the country against the French, the Scots and, later on, the Spanish. Francis Drake's ships *Greyhound* and *Pelican* (later

The Golden Hind (originally called *The Pelican*) was built at Aldeburgh and launched at the Royal Dockyard in Deptford, London. It was in this ship that Sir Francis Drake circumnavigated the globe between 1577 and 1580.
Gregory Robinson, Golden Hind, watercolour, undated, 17.8 x 25.4cm.
(National Maritime Museum)

renamed *The Golden Hind*) were built in the docks here and were among many used in the sea battles of the 1500s including most famously of all, the defeat of the Spanish Armada in 1588. The three families whose names are most associated with the Aldeburgh boatyards in those times are those of Johnson, Bence and Hunt. All of them made a long and important contribution to the history of the town.

By the 1520s boats from Aldeburgh were part of a 400-strong East Anglian fleet of fishing vessels which made regular expeditions in the North Atlantic, and their catches ensured the town grew and prospered. Fishing smacks based in Slaughden and the Haven, were fishing in Icelandic waters on lengthy six-month expeditions for at least a hundred years before Christopher Columbus 'discovered' America in 1492. The fish were preserved using Aldeburgh salt for the journey home. Their largest problem was the piratical Dunkirkers: marauding invaders from continental Europe, so named because Dunkirk had been captured so many times in the preceeding three centuries by Burgundy, Austria, Spain and France, and these pirates waited off the coast to intercept the boats and steal the catch before it could be landed.

In the early sixteenth century, the main method of shopping and trading was at the weekly market. The market-place in Aldeburgh was on the land in front of the White

Lion Hotel where there were at that time several rows of houses and streets between there and the sea. Strict rules controlled the trading in the market, designed specifically to protect the interests of the local residents and fishermen. For example, there was a habit of 'foreigners' (from other nearby towns) selling poor quality meat after dark, and so a bylaw was passed which stated that that the market should not open before sunrise, and must close four hours after midday. Later, in 1568, Elizabeth I granted Letters Patent for the town to hold a Court of Pie Powder, or Pedis Pulverisati – literally 'dusty foot' – concurrently with the market. Its purpose was to deal with debt and trespass in the market place, and as the name suggests, justice was meted out so swiftly that the litigant did not even have the time to shake the dust of the market from his feet.

An engraving of Francis Drake at Ternate in the Moluccas, November 1579. *The Golden Hind* can be seen on the left of the picture. *Gottfried*, etching, 15.3 x 17.5cm.
(National Maritime Museum)

105

English ships and the Spanish Armada. Four ships from Aldeburgh were sent to join the English fleet against the Spanish Armada in 1588. It is not clear from this painting which part of the battle is shown, but it is most likely to be the Gravelines, the only point at which large numbers of ships from both sides were engaged in sustained conflict. English school, sixteenth century (undated), oil on panel, 111.8 x 143.5cm. (National Maritime Museum)

When it was first built, the Moot Hall was open on the ground floor to accommodate market stalls. At the right-hand end was a small jail. The council chamber has always been at the top of the steps on the first floor. The chimneys were a later addition to the main structure which is more or less as it was constructed by the 1540s. On the right-hand end of the south wall there is a sundial. The brickwork of the Moot Hall is particularly distinctive.

In 1527 the State Papers of Henry VIII mention an incident in which an Aldeburgh boat was harassed by a Spanish one in the Bay of Biscay; the report states that Cardinal Wolsey made an official complaint to the Spanish Ambassador on behalf of the town. The government paper, however, fails to place the incident in the context of the great programme of espionage that was being conducted between England and Spain. Both countries were trying to embarrass the other in the question of Henry's desire to divorce Katherine of Aragon. Katherine was sending secret messages to her nephew Charles V of Spain by both sea and overland routes. Ships of both countries were stopping and searching those of the other in attempts to stop important papers passing to the lawyers on both sides.

Cardinal Wolsey found himself in an impossible position. He was not able to resolve the matter of the divorce for Henry, but neither could he appease the needs of the Pope, Charles V, or Katherine. In the end it was not Henry who forced him out of office, but the faction who supported Henry's mistress and subsequent queen, Anne Boleyn. Wolsey died, still calculating, at the moment the pendulum of power swung away from him.

A detail from the Moot Hall, highlighting the striking pattern of brickwork. Photograph by Tony Boughen, reproduced by kind permission of the photographer.

THOMAS Howard Duc et Comte de Norfolc, Comte de Surrie, Seig.r
de Howard, Moubray, Segrave, Brufe Comte, marefcffl, grand
Threforier et Admiral D'Angletrre-, et

Immediately all his estates and influences were removed. Among these was the manor of Aldeburgh and Snape, which was then granted by the King in 1536 to Thomas Howard, Duke of Norfolk and Lord High Admiral of England, and a descendant of Hugh Bigod at Framlingham. This again was a stroke of good fortune for the town. Norfolk's star would also later fall, but at this point he embarked on the creation of the status of borough for Aldeburgh and was granted the funds and permissions for the building of the Moot Hall. The borough was finally created upon the accession to the throne of Edward VI, Henry's son, in 1547, in recognition of the contribution of the town to the national fishing economy, its endeavours in the maritime defence of England, and the rising status of the local nobility.

For a while Aldeburgh was one of the most important towns of the country. Both Wolsey and Thomas Howard, Duke of Norfolk knew the town well and it is safe to assume they were regular visitors with a substantial retinue in both cases. Slaughden quay would have been an impressive site with the masts of the galleons of the King's navy swaying in the wind, just as as the sails of today's rather smaller boats do now.

Thomas Howard, 3rd Duke of Norfolk. At the time of the dissolution of the monasteries Thomas Howard acquired the manor of Aldeburgh, which then was forfeited to the Crown on his fall from power in 1546. In 1547 a charter was issued, conferring borough status on the town. Line engraving, undated, probably made by Balthasar after Hans Holbein the Younger, 15 x 10.7cm. (National Portrait Gallery)

Rob Barnes, Aldeburgh Boats, limited edition linocut. Reproduced by kind permission of the artist.

Every town and particularly every church in England was affected by the upheaval created by Henry VIII's passionate, overwhelming affair with Anne Boleyn. Henry's wife Katherine of Aragon had been a wise, and agreeable Queen who was always close to her own Spanish family. She was a devout Catholic, as was her daughter the Princess Mary. The royal marriage was initially both loving and diplomatic, but over two decades Henry's interest in Katherine declined, and when Anne Boleyn came to court in 1525, the king threw any remaining virtue away. His daughter Mary, who was twelve at the time of the attempted divorce, absolutely hated him for what he did to her mother, and it is not hard to understand why.

Mary waited through the brief reign of her stepbrother Edward and then, married to Philip King of Spain, she set about restoring a strong relationship with the Pope. England, she believed, must be Catholic, not Protestant. In only a few years she executed hundreds of Protestants throughout the country and earned her name of Bloody Mary.

In Aldeburgh, the creation of the town as a borough in 1547, and the wealth that came with shipbuilding, trading and fishing, were strong reasons to believe that Protestant Henry had been good for the town and therefore their inclination was to lie low at the time of Catholic Mary. Indeed, Henry was regarded as a national hero to the sailors and fishermen of Aldeburgh. When Mary's stepsister Elizabeth became queen in 1558 she restored the policies of her father and reaffirmed the Protestant faith. The town rejoiced and supported her: by the end of her reign her imaginary title of Gloriana – bestowed by Edmund Spenser in his 1590 poem *The Faerie Queen* – was one that Aldeburgh would have approved of: it was most definitely a pro-Elizabethan town and an anti-Catholic one.

The creation of 'The Borough' of Aldeburgh brought with it a structure of burgesses and bailiffs of which the local townspeople were vociferously dismissive. One of the enduring characteristics of the town has been the way in which the locals have largely treated authority with disdain. Two centuries later, the eighteenth-century poet George Crabbe, was masterful in the way he captured and described those relationships.

There is an Elizabethan edict in the town archive which begs the local people to be more respectful and not to sneer and ignore their newly elevated politicians, but such pleas had little effect:

> we have ordained good and wholesome laws but certain persons have wilfully threatened to break same and indecently jested, uttered and talked about in open taverns, the counsels of this town …. We hereby order for a first offence they shall be jailed and for a second they shall not be admitted to the town again.

Success and apparent prosperity meant that by the sixteenth century Aldeburgh had become very large and crowded. After the church and the Moot Hall, some of the houses at the south end of the High Street date from this period, and are amongst the oldest inhabited buildings still standing.

By 1550 the town had slightly more than 2,000 inhabitants, roughly the same number as it had in the early twenty-first century. However the population of the whole country at that time was less than 5% of ours now. Moreover Aldeburgh's population of 2,000 represented a very rapid growth since the plagues of the Black Death in the mid-fourteenth century, after which there were only 500 people in the town. This new large population faced many problems, and not just those caused by the befuddled town council. Their economy depended upon the sea for fishing and boat-building and its geographical isolation from inland Suffolk left it vulnerable to constant physical attack from other countries and particularly pirates at sea. The history of ships and cargoes lost is frightening to read.

Furthermore in the days of inadequate drainage and sewage, an isolated town bound by the sea faced the risk of plague and incurable diseases. The meticulous and beautifully handwritten church register shows several years in which more than one in six of the population died. There were a few medical practitioners in the town, but whether they were qualified or licensed is doubtful, and they had a struggle to defeat illness and disease in an artificially large and densely populated area.

Gradually the sea began to silt up the entrance to the Haven at the north of the town. This had always been a much more convenient place to lay up ships than Slaughden

Rob Barnes, On the Shingle,
limited edition linocut.
Reproduced by kind
permission of the artist.

because it could be easily accessed by the vessels coming home from the north. There was no need to divert round by Orford, where the Alde entered the ocean at that time. There was a constant and expensive attempt to dredge the opening which was around the current position of Sluice Cottage on the new road to Thorpeness. To mark the entry to the Haven there were two fiery beacons on the beach which marked the route into harbour for ships at sea.

The people of the town - or rather the Borough - appealed to Elizabeth I for financial assistance to construct sea defences. But the war against Spain meant the queen had no funds to give them, and instead the bailiffs issued a byelaw in 1590 that 'because of the sea wynnethe of the land against this towne' the inhabitants were forbidden from removing shingle from the beach 'under pain of a fine of three shillings and fourpence'. It was a sensible edict: shingle is itself the best fortification against the power of the waves. No wall is as strong. That law preventing people from removing stones from the seashore is still in force.

With so many families to feed, there was an ever present possibility of famine if the harvest failed and the fishing catch was small. In the bleak winter of 1557 when starvation and cold threatened many, the long beach known as Sudbourne down the

sea coast to Orford was miraculously covered in an edible pea plant in a greater quantity than had ever been seen before, and provided sustenance for many townsfolk.

Almost a hundred years later, a series of events in 1662 marked the end of Aldeburgh as a town that aspired to be a national sea port. After the restoration of King Charles II in 1660, engineers, architects and builders from the Continent flocked to England, and many of the great fishing towns of the east coast such as Ipswich, Hull, Whitby, Grimsby and Yarmouth made use of their newly available engineering skills and dock construction methods. Aldeburgh could certainly have been a candidate to place itself amongst those, but internal strife in the town council and the loss of money over one enterprise involving the local Johnson family and a ship, appears to have removed the will and the means of the town to prosper.

Thomas Johnson was a prosperous fisherman and his nephew John decided to embark on a major investment, to raise the funds to purchase a large fishing vessel. He called upon the burgesses of Aldeburgh to join him and take shares of the boat, *The Rainbow*, which was to be built by William Crispe of Walberswick. But young John Johnson was not as expert as his uncle had been, and the cost of the boat far exceeded the original estimate. He then tried to raise more funding by mortgaging all the immense family property in the town, but this led to a legal dispute about who would own the boat when it was finished. The whole episode ended in a high court battle in which all the parties lost large sums of money. The project was a disaster and from this point on there was no source of municipal investment in the town's shipbuilding and dock, and no grandees to undertake it. Aldeburgh was left to the ravages of the sea and naval skirmishes with the Spanish. The population dwindled back down to only a few hundred that plague and poverty had not caught.

The shingle on Aldeburgh beach is protected by a 450-year-old law from being removed by people, and is its best defence against the sea.
Graham Spice, Shingle Street. linocut, 30 x 51cm.
Reproduced by kind permission of the artist, courtesy of Aldeburgh Contemporary Arts.

CHAPTER 8:
CARVED STONES AND MARSH SPIRITS

Even now a visitor's first view of the sea at Aldeburgh is through the porch of the church as the road into the town passes it by. Ever since the earliest Roman occupation of the area, this was probably the point of strategic importance upon which the old fort 'Alde Burgh' was constructed.

It became a religious site when the Saxons turned their round lookout tower into a Christian church at around 600 AD. In order to defend the River Alde they also built a church at Iken and the first churches at Hazelwood and Snape, which are all listed in the Domesday Book. Raedwald, the Anglo Saxon King, who was local to Aldeburgh and was buried at Sutton Hoo, played an important role in bringing Christianity to England. He was a contemporary of St Augustine, the first Archbishop of Canterbury. Raedwald travelled to Kent and accepted Christianity from Augustine and made it the religion of eastern England, over which he held dominion. It is said that his wife, who did not agree with his conversion, insisted that he also maintained allegiance to the gods of his ancestors, and he was made to put two altars in his churches.

At Iken the original structure of St Botolph's Church was built on another strategic high point over a harbour in the river by the Anglo Saxons at the same time. A huge Saxon cross was mounted on top of the cliff to ward off the marsh demons and to stand visible to sailors navigating the twists of the river before the tower of the church was built. During many reconstructions this cross, placed on its side, became a lintel in a new tower; it was hued and then carved from a vast piece of stone ten feet long. It now lies on the floor of the church.

Sailors who live at the mercy of the sea have a particular need for religion. The passage through this terrain of centuries of marauders and invaders, and later of their families in search of stability and a living has left little mark on the landscape except for the stone churches and the religious institutions that grew around them. The buried ships and jewellery at Sutton Hoo and the granite carvings at Snape and Iken indicate resource, wealth and a culture to admire, but one of which we know very little. We call these the Dark Ages but one senses that they must in many respects have been golden, and undoubtedly there is much more to be discovered about this period of our history. It is frustrating that we cannot perceive the constraint or comfort they sought through their religious beliefs; their history is like an unexplored continent.

When the French came to England after the Norman Conquest, the religious structure of the country was already well-organised; priors and monks were highly educated people and were sophisticated in their ability to create well-run and often lucrative institutions.

Muslim soldiers are beseiged by Christian invaders in a tower. British Library MS Royal 16 C vi. Detail of a miniature from Chronique de France ou de Saint Denis, fourteenth century.

Andr comme ces choses à
uindrent en france: li bons

Jules George, Iken Church
(Missing you El Solido),
2006-07, oil on linen,
81 x 40cm.
Reproduced by kind
permission of the artist.

William the Conqueror portioned out control and ownership of the country to his French companions. In 1095, one William Martel, who had come over with William the Conqueror and was from one of the most renowned of French royal families, was given the manor of Aldeburgh. When William Martel senior died, the manor passed to his son, also William. The lands and properties given by the king to the Martel family included the ownership of all flotsam and jetsam on the sea shore from Thorpe to Orford. This was even more valuable than it would be now. These were perilous days of seafaring when fishermen had to cope with both the terrifying storms of the North Sea and the continuous presence of marauders from the Continent trying to steal their precious catch before it could be landed. Martel senior divided up the lands of the manor and made them into farms; he then built a priory close to the river bridge at Snape and new Norman churches at Iken and Aldeburgh using the flint and stone that had been used to build the original Saxon sanctuaries.

Young William Martel married the daughter of a local Dane. Her name was Albreda and they had a son called Geoffrey. However instead of devoting himself to the further development of the estate, Martel decided to venture across Europe and fight the Muslims in the Second Christian Crusade to the Holy Land in 1155.

Before he left, he put his wife and son into the care of the Prior of Snape and, in case he should die on his journeys, he left a will that required the monks to care for them and to provide religious services in the area. In return for carrying out these duties in his will, he gave the manor of Aldeburgh and all its lands to the Benedictine religious house of St John in Colchester. His will named the parishes at Aldeburgh, Snape, Hazelwood, Friston and Beningfield. It was the archetypal story of a knight locking up his wife to go off to fight in distant parts.

William Martel joined the French Army at Metz. At the same time, a second army in Germany comprising Saxons and other Germans assembled and set out for the Holy Land. Both were under the leadership of Pope Eugene IV.

The Second Crusade was a disaster for the Christians of Western Europe. Their armies were defeated ignominiously and many knights died. Among them, it seems, was William Martel of Aldeburgh who never returned, and whose will was executed and so the ownership of the lands upon which Aldeburgh stands passed into the hands of the religious community at Snape.

The problem was that the flotsam and jetsam on the beach were such a source of wealth that the monks of Snape did not concentrate either on developing the land and the religious buildings or on their religious duties with the same thoroughness as their neighbours, particularly the Prior of Butley, near Orford to the south, or Leiston to the north.

The ruins of Leiston Abbey, built as an Augustinian foundation in 1182.
(Mary Evans Picture Library)

If William Martel had returned home from the Crusades and managed the lands himself it would have been better not only for his family, but for the whole town. The manor of Aldeburgh was not in good care after its early days and that neglect has left its mark on the town.

The construction of the Norman churches required a major development of the surrounding area, and the monks at Snape built a water-mill, a dam, priory buildings and a bridge over the river, the first since the Romans had left and close to where the current bridge stands. That piece of engineering changed the nature of the river from Snape westwards. The religious community at Snape obtained substantial income from all the parishes, their own lands and the mill. They were also in demand as copiers and scriveners, being educated in Latin and handwriting. Where most other individuals in the area worked entirely for themselves or a few at the whim of a rich landowner, the monks of Snape Priory and Aldeburgh Manor had established a stable industry and security that required no physical labour. More than that, they had the means and the methods of taking a share in other people's wealth and income, through their churches and parishes and through the rich pickings of the beach.

It may have been these reasons that led the priors of Snape to ignore the opportunity taken by all around them to participate in the development of the wool trade in and around Aldeburgh.

In the twelfth and thirteenth century Butley Priory used dyke builders from Holland to create a set of sea walls that turned the marshes from Havergate Island to the south of the Alde into fine grazing land for sheep. These sea walls still stand, and today provide walkways along the coast. By these means the priory of Butley and Orford became prosperous in a way that Aldeburgh did not. The wool trade in Suffolk was one of the most important economic developments for centuries and Aldeburgh stood on the edge of it with only a passing involvement in the shipping of exports from Slaughden and the beach.

The list of priors of Snape after John Colchester shows how the educated classes of the country had become French: de Neyland, de Elyton, de Colne, de Colne, de Bury, de Grensted, de Mersey and so on.

In 1400 a warrant for the arrest of the John de Mersey was issued by King Henry IV for attempting to make Snape Priory independent of Colchester and the jurisdiction of the King, and take it under the direct rule of Rome. A papal bull, or edict, had been issued by Pope Boniface IX granting separation after Isabel, Countess of Suffolk and patroness of the priory, complained that the abbey and convent of Colchester did not maintain enough religious persons at Snape, as they were ordained to do. The King, when he was told, was furious at this blatant side-stepping of his authority and issued warrants for

Colin Slee, The Alde, 2011, acrylic on canvas, 70 x 100cm. Reproduced by kind permission of the artist.

de Mersey to be tried in the court of Chancery and prevented from leaving the country. De Mersey went into hiding and was never brought in front of the King and there is no further record of him. It was to counter exactly this kind of Papal interference that the law of Praemunire was created. The case of de Mersey was a foretaste of a legal and moral battle that would be fought hard across the country during the next hundred years: was the loyalty of a churchman or woman first to the Pope or to the King? Whereas there had been no difficulty in such questions in 1150 for Martel, a conflict of allegiances had arisen over the succeeding years. The Church appeared to set itself above the constitutional laws, and had clearly become more and more disdainful of common people, as the activities at Snape Priory demonstrated.

Nevertheless in 1446, by Papal edict, the successors of John de Mersey finally won their independence from Colchester Abbey and from the King of England. For two years Snape and Aldeburgh was no longer answerable or required to pay taxes to the King of England but instead they went to Pope Eugenius IV in Rome.

With the power this gave them, the priors of Snape imposed a mighty tax on the fishermen of Aldeburgh. Every boat that fished at the time of spratting was required to pay a tax of ten shillings to the Priory. Unsurprisingly, this caused enormous strife and poverty in the town.

Two years after its instigation, the tax was withdrawn. Goodness knows how the townspeople made the strength of their feelings known, but the Prior Dannibregge reduced the levy to just two pence per boat. He must have been under some intense pressure. One imagines riots and violent actions by the fishermen or even their wives who were faced with poverty whilst their men were at sea, but there is no record of the form that the lobbying from the local people or their possible revolt took. This kind of event shows how, just eighty years later, Henry VIII became so popular among ordinary people when he sought to reform and remove the powers of the church in England and the people's allegiance to the Pope.

When, on the instruction of Cardinal Wolsey, the tax on spratting was eventually removed in its entirety, the fishermen of Aldeburgh promised thereafter to send an annual gift of sprats to the Mayor of London, a practice which continues to this day.

It was for the purpose of building a college in Ipswich that Wolsey took over the rights and incomes of the priory of Snape and with it the Manor of Aldeburgh. This was the time at which Wolsey also commandeered the income of many monasteries and priories in order to build his great colleges in Oxford and Cambridge. Throughout the whole previous century the people of Aldeburgh had sided with whomever was King, primarily to object to the bullying behaviour of the priors of Snape. This act by Wolsey and Henry VIII in unified defiance of the religious order was very welcome and was accompanied by favours of boat building. Between 1520 and 1540 it also brought the construction of a fine Moot Hall from which the council officials of the town could conduct their affairs.

Janet Judge, Silver Sprats, watercolour, 35 x 25cm.
Reproduced by kind permission of the artist,
courtesy of Aldeburgh Contemporary Arts.

John Piper, Aldeburgh Church. The painting still hangs in Britten's bedroom in The Red House. Reproduced by permission of the estate of John Piper and courtesy of the Britten Pears Foundation.

For a long time, across the whole of Christian Europe, the rapacious and unfair dominance of religious houses under the pretext of the will of God had caused deep resentment amongst working people. The Reformation, loudly and stubbornly advocated by Martin Luther in Germany was an expression of popular sentiment across northern Europe, and eventually echoed not only by kings and princes, but also by the Pope and many of his cardinals. The orders calling for the dissolution of monasteries in England were signed, not by Henry VIII, but by the Pope. In fact in the 'Great Matter' of the application for Henry's divorce from Katherine of Aragon, the one thing about which the Pope, Henry and Wolsey all agreed was the need for the destruction of the power of the abbots and priors, and the removal of their corrupt income. This was nothing to do with the division that eventually arose about whether the King or the Pope was head of the English Church, but it was a difficult and serious revaluation of the nature of power derived from religious fanaticism.

The disagreement with Luther was about whether the revolution was to be led by the people or by the monarchs — the need for church reform was not doubted, certainly not by the English, Germans and other nations of northern Europe.

In Henry VIII's time, Aldeburgh Church was enlarged and decorated, the north and south aisles were built and a lookout point was placed on the tower. In Elizabeth I's early years the Catholic symbols were removed, in the superstitious belief that failure to destroy them was a continuing cause of plague in the town. Catholicism and Papist ornamentations were banished from Aldeburgh for over three hundred years.

121

The Spanish response to the activities of firstly Henry VIII, then Elizabeth, came in the form of the invading Armada of 1588. Aldeburgh played a proud part in the defeat of the supposedly superior Iberian forces – its ships were in action up and down the east coast and into the English Channel.

Finally for Aldeburgh there was a period of peace and culture. Learning and pleasure became important – the church hosted mystery plays, and travelling musicians and actors played to the congregation. Although the Lord Chamberlain's accounts of plays and performances from 1595 to 1625 are missing, it is widely believed that the King's Players – of whom William Shakespeare was a member – visited Dunwich, and if we can accept that, then it seems quite likely that they also visited Aldeburgh. Audiences watched from the new north and south side aisles while the players performed in the centre of the nave of the church.

The Church of St Peter and St Paul itself became a vibrant centre of the prosperous market town. High above the flimsy wooden constructions of the fishermen's dwellings that stood close to the sea, its fine stone construction must have been a robust, warm and welcoming haven.

In 1619 Robert Topcliffe was appointed vicar of the church and remained in his post for twenty-five years. Once again the religious mood of the country was shifting away from the calm waters of Elizabethan Protestantism and polarising either towards the

Catholicism of the new queen, Henrietta Maria of France, or to the opposing harsh dogmas of the Puritans. Reverend Topcliffe appears to have leaned towards the sentiments of the Old Catholic papacy and followed the guidance of Archbishop Laud. He rearranged the furnishing of the church into a Roman style with a new and expensive pulpit and an altar distant from the congregation.

However others in the town took an opposing view. Thomas Johnson was a powerful businessman at that time in Aldeburgh, and whether by inclination or by a sense of expediency, he took sides with the Parliamentarians and their Puritan ideology against the King. Johnson's ally, Squire Bence, was the Member of Parliament for the town when the King purged the House of Commons. Johnson had been sent by the town to London when he was in his thirties to plead for money for defence against foreign marauders and came back with £62 and 15 shillings which he used to construct new military defences along the beach.

Ten years later, though, in 1634, Charles I had raised a tax called 'Ship Money' which forced the coastal towns of England to pay to support the national navy. This forced Aldeburgh to return the money that Johnson had raised, to the fury of the town bailiffs. As this tax was spread to inland towns it became one of the provocative acts that brought the country to civil war. In 1641 Parliament called the imposition of 'Ship Money' illegal, and that led to the first battles between the armies of the King and Parliament. The civil war of the 1640s was an extraordinary time for the town. East Anglia became

An image from the 1964 performance of *Curlew River*, an opera by Benjamin Britten, written as a modern mystery play for church performance. It evokes not only the locality of the river Alde but also much of the atmosphere of the medieval performances and is the kind of drama that was played in the church in Aldeburgh in the 1500s during the reign of Queen Elizabeth I. © Dominic Photography, courtesy of Britten-Pears Foundation.

James Dodds, Catching the Wildman, 1995, woodcut, 28 x 28cm. Reproduced by kind permission of the artist.

known as a Puritan stronghold, but it is unlikely that the ordinary people in Aldeburgh were so extreme. The Reverend Topcliffe was well-liked. While the wealthy and the important citizens like Johnson, Bence and other town burgesses, who had profited from former royal largesse, were ready to take arms against the King, the ordinary townspeople, who had benefited less themselves, were less inclined to such upheaval and had to be bullied into supporting the political aspirations of the town leaders. Topcliffe strove to bring harmony among the religious factions in the small town and to keep the church at the centre of the whole community. Whatever the ideological arguments were that divided the political classes, the church, he believed had a simpler role: to look after people and be a force for good in the community.

As if to awake and alert the inhabitants to the events, a large meteorite landed near Snape in 1641, accompanied by ferocious sound and weather. Johnson's account to the Burgesses said:

> A syne from heaven and Fearfull and Terrible noise: the beating of drums and discharging of muskets and great ordnance for an hour and more — a stone fell from the sky and is here to be seen in the towne of great weight.

In fact during the early 1600s there were a number of meteor showers observed in other parts of the world, but there was no consistent explanation of them. Johnson used the event to frighten the unwilling townspeople into joining his drill sessions for the Parliamentary army.

A year earlier in 1640 the House of Commons appointed a committee as a Court of Inquisition for members of the clergy who were considered to be 'scandalous ministers'. This enforced endorsement of puritanism manifested itself in Aldeburgh in the person of William Dowsing, a Suffolk man appointed as 'Commissioner for the destruction of monuments of idolatry and superstition' and who arrived in Aldeburgh determined to cleanse the church. With the support of Johnson and the town bailiffs, Dowsing took

James Dodds, Wildman of the Sea, 1997, linocut, 76 x 48cm. Reproduced by kind permission of the artist.

In 1641 a meteorite landed near
Snape, accompanied by terrible storms.
Elizabeth Morris, The Washing Line
and the Comet, etching and aquatint,
14 x 20cm.
Reproduced by kind permission
of the artist.

down and destroyed twenty carvings and thirty-eight paintings. The walls of the church were whitewashed: literally and figuratively, the colour of the church was erased. Topcliffe was removed from his tenure and died the next year, but the people of the town looked after his widow with kindness for many years. Both husband and wife are buried in the graveyard.

In hindsight Robert Topcliffe and his wife should be placed in the pantheon of great people of the town. Their story is of kind and cultured reconciliation wiped out by ruthless brutality, the damage from which has never been made good. Suffolk is extraordinarily rich in beautiful stone-built churches, many of them designed by Saxons before the French invasion of the eleventh century. Their purpose was much wider than we would recognise now as centres and havens for people in the vicinity. Often they were the only properly roofed and heated buildings accessible to a community where most people lived in poorly constructed dwellings. The church was the place of comfort, entertainment, education, community, as well as the wisdom and the understanding that religion brought.

William Dowsing maliciously ripped out thousands of works of art in Suffolk and Cambridgeshire churches. In Aldeburgh, aided by Thomas Johnson, his destruction of the interior of the church marked the end of its role as the centrepoint of the local community.

Johnson, in contrast to Topcliffe, is undoubtedly on the list of people who have done great harm both to the people and to the reputation and prosperity of the borough, and there was worse to come from him and from his family. Next it was the women of the town who faced an outrageous assault with the horrific assertions that many of them were witches.

In 1645 a man called Matthew Hopkins appointed himself 'Witch Finder' for Parliament and claimed that by various examinations he could identify women who were witches. Hopkins' methods are disgusting to read. The most common accusation he made against a woman was that she had an extra pap with which she fed her imps. Some witches, he said, had five imps they could call to protect them and they all came from the devil.

Aldeburgh did not escape the witch trials in East Anglia, and seven women were accused and found guilty of witchcraft in 1646. This illustration is from an earlier English pamphlet of 1589 and depicts the hanging of three Essex women: Joan Prentice, Joan Cony and Joan Upney. (Scala Images)

When he suspected a woman of witchcraft, Hopkins would keep her from sleeping for two or three days and search her body for marks of evidence — although in the living conditions of the time, what he found could have been anything: warts, abrasions or bites from bugs that infested the prison bedding. This sleep deprivation, Hopkins said, would cause a witch to call out her imps. He also claimed that because the devil was alien to water, a witch would float if she was immersed. If she sank she was innocent, although obviously by that point the accused woman would have drowned, especially as he took the precaution of tying the woman's thumbs to her opposite feet. In Aldeburgh, the

burgesses employed Hopkins to search out any witches. Seven local women were incarcerated in the Moot Hall prison in one of the coldest winters on record. Eventually, worn down by cold and exhaustion, they confessed and were hanged in February 1646. It must have been a terrifying few months for the women of a town where many of the men were away at sea and unable to protect their wives or the other women. Nonetheless, Aldeburgh may have got off lightly: in Chelmsford, Hopkins hanged nineteen women in one day.

Thomas Johnson had by this point become firstly an agent and then a Captain of the Parliamentary Army under General Fairfax. He was the burgess when large sums of money were paid from town funds to support the witch hunts of Matthew Hopkins, and it has to be supposed that in these circumstances Johnson overtly supported the intimidation of the women of his own town. He may even have been responsible for initiating it. The turmoil of revolution and civil war cause the ambitious to act against their own kind.

However if his intention by these acts was somehow to promote the town in Cromwell's regime, he failed. Dutch pirates took advantage of the domestic upheavals of the English Civil War to mount an attack on the east coast, and the consequence of their destruction was that by 1641 the population of Aldeburgh had fallen to less than 800 people.

Johnson died in 1658 and is buried in the church. His relatives then tried to extract money from the town for their own business ventures, and their greed hastened the end of the town's prosperity as a naval base. The English Civil War was a turning point for Aldeburgh, and there was no more religious development in the town for nearly two hundred years until a Baptist church was built in the early nineteenth century.

When a Catholic church was finally constructed in the 1930s it was wisely built on the top of the cliff just by the town steps. However no one could have foreseen that its Saxon-inspired round tower would be destroyed within a decade by German bombing. Since the end of the Second World War, the church of St Peter and St Paul has thrived. It remains, with the Moot Hall, one of the two most active Tudor buildings in England. Furthermore, Benjamin Britten's use of it as a venue for the Aldeburgh festival restored it to its other historic use as a cultural centre for the community.

Alan Bridges, Aldeburgh Rooftops.
Reproduced by kind permission of the artist.

CHAPTER 9:
VICTORIANS AND EDWARDIANS

For more than a hundred years after the English Civil War of the 1640s, Aldeburgh was in decline. The town fell into the damp despond and petty town squabbles that are so clearly described in the poems of George Crabbe. It was only towards the end of the eighteenth century that economic salvation began to arrive in Aldeburgh in the form of wealthy landowners who built a number of large houses above the shoreline and who, in turn attracted visitors (and their money) to the town.

The three big houses of the late eighteenth century are those built by Crespigny, at the south end of the town overlooking the estuary, and Thellusson and Wyndham just below the church. These houses still bear the names of their builders and they sit alongside the existing large houses of the prominent local Wentworth family and Aldeburgh's most famous architectural antecedents: the Moot Hall and the church. The High Street had humble fishermen's cottages in the same style as we see today. The heart of the town and its road layout has remained unchanged for as long as almost any town in England. To the south of the town, the construction of the Martello Tower in 1804 as part of the defences against Napoleon was an industry on its own. All these developments helped to enhance the natural attractions of the town and they brought the first casual visitors who rented rooms for their vacations.

Crabbe, writing in the early 1800s, also characterised the new wealthy and intellectual holidaymakers who must have appeared to have strange ways to the older inhabitants. Aldeburgh residents would not have contemplated bathing in the sea. His ironic but accurate descriptions could have been written two hundred years later - and probably will always ring true.

The story of the case of Jarndyce and Jarndyce in *Bleak House* was based on the will of Peter Thellusson of Aldeburgh. Cover of the serialised edition of *Bleak House* by Charles Dickens (British Library)

> Awhile we stop, discourse of wind and tide
> Bathing and books, the raffle and the ride
> Thus, with the aid that shops and sailing give
> Life passes on: tis labour, but we live.

Those who stroll on Crag Path today, or sit in a café to read the morning newspaper can recognise the place and the morning air from Crabbe's simple words.

Thellusson House has an interesting story to tell arising from the will of Peter Thellusson in 1797. This gentleman was a merchant who had a large personal fortune derived from a portfolio of properties from which he earned substantial annual amounts. When he

132

Peggy Somerville, Promenade, Aldeburgh, c.1960, pastel, 280 x 181cm.
The stylish mother (or nanny) approaches the south end of the Crag Path, Aldeburgh.
Reproduced by kind permisson of the Somerville estate.

Aldeburgh High Street in 1909.
(Francis Frith Collection)

died he directed that the rents from his properties were to be accumulated so they would be inherited by the next generation after his children. His sons received £600,000 but the fortune to be shared among their children amounted to £14 million.

However by the time these children came to inherit, fifty years later, a dispute arose as to who exactly were the correct beneficiaries of the will, and how the money should be shared. An act of parliament 'The Thellusson Act' of 1800 decreed that bequests of this kind should not be made, but that did not overrule what old Mr Thellusson had done. It was merely to prevent a recurrence of the confusion he had caused. The case went to the Court of Chancery and stayed there during prolonged pleading by many parties, including Lord Rendlesham and Charles Sabine Augustus Thellusson.

This court case forms the basis of the story of Jarndyce and Jarndyce as told by Charles Dickens in *Bleak House*. Dickens was present at the Thellusson hearings in the Court of Chancery, and much of his novel is devoted to a mockery of the unnecessarily complicated proceedings. In Jarndyce and Jarndyce, as was the case with Peter Thellusson's will, by the time the case was finally settled there was no money left. Every penny had gone to the lawyers.

1804 brought the construction of the monumental line of twenty-nine defensive Martello Towers along the East Anglian coast of which the Aldeburgh tower is the largest and the

134

John Bawtree, Crag Path, Aldeburgh, 2002, oil on board, 45 x 60cm. Reproduced by kind permission of the artist.

most northerly. It was built on a spit of land to the south of the town, and was constructed of over 700,000 London bricks which were brought to the site by barge. The walls on the seaward side are thirteen feet thick. During its life it has been modified to be used as a house, although between the wars it was known as a secret meeting place for lovers. Napoleon's defeat at Trafalgar in 1804 and later at Waterloo in 1815, meant the towers were not called into use at that time, however they later acted as gun emplacements in both world wars.

Early paintings of the 1800s show Crag Path as a rough track that runs along the top of the beach in front of the line of houses that were built facing the sea. Other seaside towns have developed the promenade along the sea front as a place for cafes and shops but Aldeburgh has resisted that development. There was once a sweet and toy shop owned and run by Millie Burwood but that has now been replaced by two small flats. Fishing boats and fishermen are allowed to ply their trade and sell their wares from the beach, and there are a few hotels and the lifeboat shop, but otherwise the front at Aldeburgh is free of commerce.

Race meetings at Snape racecourse were a regular feature of the early nineteenth century. There is no sign any longer of the racetrack, which lay on the north side of the river to the east of Snape Bridge, on the path of the avenue of trees from the Wentworths' house at Friston Hall southwards. Local records show this was the route to

135

Chrissy Norman, South Tower
Steps, Aldeburgh, etching,
10 x 20cm.
Reproduced by kind
permission of the artist.

the racecourse used by the prominent Wentworth family and their friends. The area of raised land is now known as Snape Warren.

In the first half of the nineteenth century before roads were 'Macadamised' and before the railway network was extended everywhere, boats were the main means of transport. London was the one of the great centres of trade, and it was on the river Thames that most of the transfer of goods took place. The central channel of river was a continuous bustle of great sailing ships and 'lighters' used to move the goods between them and to shore.

As far out of the Thames estuary as Aldeburgh, there was a continuous passage of boats carrying goods to and from the city. Vessels leaving Aldeburgh for London took on pilots to navigate the channels and sandbanks of the coast, and for their safe passage in and out of the harbour two rival lookout towers were built: the north tower 'Up-Town' for one pilot company and the south tower for the 'Down-Town' rival. Whichever company could get its pilot to a passing vessel, would win the fee. At the same time the watch-room of the Lloyds shipping register was constructed. In it the certified registrar kept a daily log of all passing boats seen through his telescope and sent the information each night by road mail to Lloyds' office in London.

Aside from visitors, prosperity came to the area in the early nineteenth century through the business acumen and enterprise of Richard Garrett. The fifth generation of the Garrett family, Richard was responsible for the building of a huge factory and ironworks around Leiston, which provided hundreds of jobs for the area and alongside it an infrastructure of schools, shops and medical care. He was one of a number of Victorian industrial magnates for whom one of the key components for the success of their business was a large, loyal and dependent labour force who lived around the factory works.

The local school in Leiston was important to Garrett Engineering as a source of skilled labour. An industry of such scale needed properly trained toolmakers, draughtsmen, engineers and designers, as well as salesmen and administrators to conduct negotiations with governments around the world.

One of the expansionist strategies of the British Empire was to lend money to foreign rulers with the requirement that it was spent on infrastructure and engineering projects of the kind with which British companies such as Garrett's were closely involved. A jungle road, desert crossing or railway needed traction engines of the kind built in the Leiston engineering works. For a rural agricultural community to produce a world-class business enterprise was a triumph. Success of this kind is not all about finger wagging at the boardroom table. Long apprenticeships require more than hours at a lathe or in a forge; they need a full educational programme in administration, language and numerical skills. This is why the schools in Aldeburgh were for a hundred years inferior to their counterparts

The Garrett & Son exhibit in the Agricultural Court at the 1851 Great Exhibition, Crystal Palace, London. The plate was included in the catalogue for the exhibition, and the caption read 'Richard Garrett & Son have recently arranged for the manufacture of steam cultivating apparatus with the latest improvements, under Messrs. Howard's various patents.' C. T. Dolby, 1851, coloured lithograph.
(The Stapleton Collection/Bridgeman Art Library)

A Garrett steam road locomotive, 1910. North Eastern Railways engine no. 108, hauling a thirty-ton industrial boiler. (National Railway Museum/ Science & Society Photo Library)

in Leiston. Teaching of a very high standard took place under the careful eye of Garrett's family, and Richard Garrett himself went on to found Framlingham School. Nowadays we assume the government will take responsibility for educating every new generation. At that time it was often the local industrialists who undertook the work (alongside church schools) both for the benefit it brought their business and as part of their own contribution to the general advancement of their community.

Because of the consistently high educational standards at Leiston in the nineteenth and early twentieth century, Aldeburgh pupils were frequently sent to school there. School records are still in the Moot Hall and the names of children, teachers and governors are easily recognised: Ward, Marjoram and Philpott were sent home to have their hair de-loused, and Ivy Philpott's mother was to be prosecuted by Dr Savage and the school for the louse-infested state of her daughter's head. Miss Todd, the teacher, was frequently absent because of a cold. Mr Burwood was an inspector. Eighteen girls attended cookery classes in Leiston.

Angela Burdett-Coutts, an illustration from the periodical 'Vanity Fair'. Coloured lithograph. (Wimbledon Society Museum/ Bridgeman Art Library)

Into the Victorian world of aristocrats, fishermen and entrepreneurs, came a clergyman called Henry Thompson and his wife Georgie. Fortunately for modern historians, Georgie kept a diary, and amongst her entries is the story of a blind child from Hazelwood called Willie Cook. Georgie had discovered on her parish visits that Willie had a particular affinity for music. He loved to hear it played and begged to be taken to any concert or recital.

Georgie Thompson had met Baroness Burdett-Coutts on an occasion when she came to stay in the town with her husband. They had talked about the needs of the poor and after she left, Georgie wrote to her and told her about the particular musical interests of little Willie Cook.

The Burdett-Coutts are one of the best endowed families of England, owning banks and international companies and Angela Georgina Burdett-Coutts was simply the richest woman in the country. She did not marry until she was sixty-seven and her husband, who was American and had previously been her secretary, was forty years younger. Their marriage caused a considerable sensation. The couple stayed in Aldeburgh at the White Lion Hotel, after their wedding.

After receiving Georgie's letter, Mrs Burdett-Coutts sent a magnificent music box as a special present to little Willie Cook of Hazelwood. The mechanism was mounted in a glass box and could be set in motion by the blind boy. It played several tunes and was inscribed with a personal message. Georgie Thompson reported in her diary that the present of the music box gave more pleasure than any other gift the great lady ever made. Baroness Burdett-Coutts was an exceptional philanthropist who gave away the equivalent of 300 million pounds in her lifetime, at today's values. The Prince of Wales, later King Edward VII, described her as 'the second lady in the kingdom after my mother'.

The small parts assembly shop at Garrett's foundry in Leiston, 1925. Small parts were made into larger assemblies for fitting to the products. Parts for steam engines can also be seen in this view. Private collection, reproduced by kind permission of Michael Walters.

Edward VII was inclined to gamble, and led a somewhat wayward social life as a young man. It is said that he used the Royal Yacht for making visits to Aldeburgh, and that he played cards in Edinburgh House which is on the sea front close to the Jubilee Hall.

Elsewhere in her diary Georgie described Mr Marjoram the chimney sweep who lived in the Old Custom House on the High Street. Before he moved in the house had recently been used as a parish-room in which Georgie Thompson held meetings for mothers of the parish. Her daughter Dorothy later described the old house as having a 'fair sized room entered by a flight of steps from the street and underneath was like a cave that was said to have been used by smugglers'. Mr and Mrs Marjoram set up their sign on the door:

> Marjoram the Sweep lives here
> He sweeps the chimneys far and near
> And when by chance they catch alight
> He'll put them out at your desire

Marjoram's donkey pulled a cart and Dorothy Thompson recorded that sweeping chimneys was thirsty work, as the donkey was accustomed to call in at 'places of refreshment'.

Crespigny House proved a difficult investment. The Crespigny family were forced to sell it not long after completing the building and in 1895 it became a private grammar school until the school moved to Eaton House, the fine building behind the Wentworth Hotel. Later on the school was moved to Orwell Park outside Ipswich where it still operates.

The industrial revival of Aldeburgh continued with the 1843 discovery by Mr Edward Packard of a lucrative use for a local underground mineral, which gave rise to the so-called 'Aldeburgh Gold Rush'. Crag is the stone found in the fields around Aldeburgh that can be used to make pathways, but the Victorians discovered that in the layer underneath the crag was a material which could be used as highly effective fertilizer. It was found in seams from Aldeburgh to Orford and mined wherever it could be uncovered. The proceeds from the sale of phosphates quickly made many local people very rich. It could be sold for the equivalent of £250 per ton and a one-acre field could produce 300 tons. For thirty years Newson Garrett and other local entrepreneurs who hurried to buy land in the area were able to profit at the rate of £75,000 per acre wherever they could obtain the mining rights.

This discovery was the beginning of the phosphate industry for which Fisons of Felixstowe eventually became known around the world, but it all started in Saxmundham and Snape. In the papers that speculate the exact detail of Mr Packard's work it states that he may have used the small mill in Snape that stands just north of the river bridge as a place to grind the stone. Others dismiss that theory in favour of the more probable

Crespigny House, 1855. Built in the eighteenth century with stunning views to the south of the town, the house has had a chequered history and been used for many purposes, including as a grammar school. In this engraving a cricket match is being played in the grounds.

idea that most of the work took place within Snape Maltings. That small mill at the time belonged to a Mr Hudson and was in fact used for the production of 'superior' white flour until the 1930s, whereupon it became even more famous when it was purchased by a young musical composer called Benjamin Britten.

The Aldeburgh vicar at this time, Henry Thompson, dealt with several difficult cases in which employment at sea brought strains at home. One such involved a fisherman who, having spent most of the year away at sea trawling in the waters off Iceland, came home to find that his wife had become pregnant in his absence.

No word was ever said and not long after the birth, his wife died. The man made no comment at all but gave up his life at sea to take care of his adopted daughter and give her an education. Others in the town knew what had happened, but no one ever mentioned the matter out of respect for him and the girl. He became a labourer in the fields and his life was hard but he never sought out the other man nor pursued revenge.

In her book *Sophia's Son,* Henry Thompson's daughter Dorothy records the arrival of gas and water to the town in the last years of the century. The first motor car in Aldeburgh in the early twentieth century belonged to the Vernon Wentworth family and it came to collect the vicar and his wife to take them to lunch in Hazelwood. Dorothy Thompson wrote that her mother was totally terrified by the idea of going in the motor, but she told her children that 'if their father was to die in the adventure, then it were better that she should go, too'.

Trevor Woods, Sizewell Beach, 2009, acrylic and ink on heavyweight watercolour paper, 26 x 37cm.
Reproduced by kind permission of the artist, courtesy of Aldeburgh Contemporary Arts.

Dorothy also records the sad loss of the town lifeboat in 1899 with a description of the funeral of the brave men:

'all through the night before the snow fell softly and the churchyard was covered with a pure white glistening carpet; paths had to be swept and sanded, but all around lay a white pall. Business was suspended, shops shut, flags flown at half mast. One by one the six coffins, covered with Union Jacks, were borne on hand biers from their cottage homes into the main street. The lifeboat crew in life belts and scarlet caps were ready to receive them and act as pall bearers.

The graves are each marked with a little white marble cross, all alike, and there are seven of them (one man died later) and there is a memorial in the church, a beautiful bronze of the lifeboat making her way through heavy seas. It commemorates heroes of a deed as brave as any done in heat of battle.'

It was a sad end to the century for Aldeburgh.

The First World War brought about the decline of Garrett's of Leiston. For years Garrett's had built engines to supply the vast farming needs of Russia as well as farming enterprises nearer to home. But as the great revolutionary conflict deepened, the Russian government, overburdened by huge costs, became unwilling to pay the money they owed abroad. Matters worsened when the Soviet government of 1917 took ownership of all agricultural machinery and refused to pay any outstanding debts. Garrett's of Leiston lost £200,000 in cash. This catastrophic event coincided with other changes in the international market brought about by the end of the war in 1918. American manufacturers were not only technically advanced, but they had access to easy credit and economies of scale that outstripped those in Britain. The shift in the balance of industrialized power was an abrupt change, for which rural Suffolk (and indeed the whole of Britain) was ill-prepared and against which it had no defence. Richard Garrett's firm was forced into liquidation and although there were several attempts at diversification by different owners, the heart had gone from the business and eventually the factories were closed down. The redundancy of such a sizeable number of people brought great poverty to Leiston and to the surrounding towns including Aldeburgh. It was a sad end to many proud years of ingenious agricultural and heavy engineering. The museum in Leiston tells the story as a testament not only to the innovative engineering processes and products, but also to the Victorian heritage of a family at work. In Leiston, and indeed throughout England, almost nothing is left of the age of cast iron and oily pistons. Yet for a hundred and fifty years or more, Garrett Engineering was a vital part of the life and economy of this part of British industry, and its machinery had helped to develop farming methods throughout the world.

Richard Garrett's house was sold in 1920 to an educational iconclast called A. S. Neill, who turned it into a school called Summerhill, which continues to attract headlines to this day. Neill's groundbreaking theory of learning was that the school should fit the child rather than the other way around, and he wrote 'I would rather Summerhill produced a happy street cleaner than a neurotic scholar'. As a result the school was (and is) often perceived to be a place where pupils have free reign to behave as they like. This is not quite the case. Pupils do indeed make the rules, but they conform to them, and the school has a credible list of alumni, particularly in the fields of art and drama, for example the artists Ishbel McWhirter and Evelyn Williams.

Leiston in the 1960s became a centre for another kind of engineering, and its railway remained in use as a carrier for the nuclear power station on Sizewell beach.

Wilfred Williams Ball, Study of a Watermeadow Scene near Aldeburgh,1911, watercolour, 26 x 45cm.
Private collection, reproduced courtesy of Abbots Countrywide.

Aldeburgh has also been host to one of the most fascinating technical advances: the electric telegraph. There are three brightly coloured telegraph poles in the town that mark the English end of an underwater cable that connects the mainland to the nineteenth-century network of telegraph lines. In the 1840s Professor Wheatstone discovered that you could send electronic forms of messages down a long cable 'with great rapidity and discretion'. Very quickly, both industry (particularly newspapers) and governments with financial and military interests recognised the value of this, and responded to create a network of telegraphic cables around the world.

There were five windmills in Aldeburgh in the nineteenth century. Three of them had been there for over three hundred years. To the north the Haven was drained by a windmill. A second stood by the church. There were two more on the terrace by Alde House and Crespigny House and the fifth can still be seen on the seafront at the south of the town. It no longer has its sails, but the tower is evident.

We forget how dependent a seaside town was on its ability to harness the wind, both in the sailing of ships and in the power of the pump or the grindstone of the windmill. Those forms of industrial technology are gone, but the principles of wind-based sources of power have been rediscovered by new generations of engineers, who have built huge farms of wind turbines which now stand sentinel along the Suffolk coast, harnessing the power of the offshore winds to create energy.

Another industrial phenomenon that is sadly in decline is the manned lighthouse which provides direction and illumination for those at sea, and additionally watches for and monitors shipping vessels in the locality. The lighthouse at Orford Ness still shines, but its days are numbered as it has been de-commissioned, along with many others. Originally there were two lighthouses standing, one due east of the other, so that when lined up from sea they indicated the latitude of a ship. Aldeburgh church tower has also been used as a lookout and a beacon as have Orford Castle and the Martello Tower.

Right: *Penny Bhadresa*, Orford Ness, 2009, linocut, 14 x 13cm. Reproduced by kind permission of the artist.

Below: *William Daniell,* Orford Ness Lighthouse, 1822, aquatint. From Volume VI of 'A Voyage Around Great Britain Undertaken between the years 1814 and 1825' by William Daniell. (Namur Archive/Scala Images)

The Orford Ness Light houses, Suffolk.

A scene on the sea front, 1900. The South Tower is just visible in the distance.
(Francis Frith Collection)

For just one hundred years the railway played a significant role in the town's history. Many English towns have suffered from the terrible reduction of the railway network in the 1960s, and Aldeburgh still feels the sad loss. It is not hard to imagine how popular and well-used the railway would be, if the line from Saxmundham to Leiston and Aldeburgh was still in operation. There are only sepia photographs and a few films that record the beautiful Victorian station and 'The Aldeburgh Flier' that shuttled to and fro between the towns.

Both the development of the railway and the improved surfacing of roads began to affect the volume of goods carried by ship. As the inland transport infrastructure improved, it became clear that the North Sea was no longer the most efficient way of transporting goods between the north and east of England and London, and the railway took over as the preferred means of moving goods and materials.

It was not just industry that made use of the new trains. Long before motor cars were invented, steam trains made it possible for ever-increasing numbers of people to come from London and the cities to the seaside. A visit to the beach was no longer just for the rich or adventurous traveller. It created an opportunity for families or even individuals in need of rest and relaxation.

Travellers needed hotels and guest houses, beach facilities and diversions for their children. In response to the growing numbers of visitors to the town, Aldeburgh council built a pier which reached into the sea opposite the White Lion Hotel. Unfortunately, unlike the piers in Southwold and Felixstowe, the Aldeburgh pier was built with considerably less skill and enthusiasm than those of its neighbours. It reached only a few feet out to sea and stood unfinished for many years and was rather a hazard for passing boats. Those late Victorian days also saw a plethora of bathing machines and other paraphernalia on the beach.

148

Yet Aldeburgh seafront has always belonged truly to the fishermen. Even at the height of Victorian holidaymaking it remained essentially a working beach, the fishing boats sitting uncomfortably alongside families with wind-breakers, towels and bathing costumes. The holidaymakers have no option but to deal with oily winches, smelly nets, fishing tackle, splintered boats and uncomfortable shingle. That is why the place retains its character.

ALDEBURGH
FOR A CULTURED SEASIDE EXPERIENCE

Amelia Bowman, Aldeburgh – for a Cultured Seaside Experience, 2012, digitally reproduced collagraph print, 43 x 40cm. Reproduced by kind permission of the artist.

CHAPTER 10:

THE WENTWORTHS AND THE GARRETTS

DYNASTIES AND POLITICS

The first Earl of Strafford (1593–1641). Contemporary line engraving, after Sir Anthony van Dyck (National Portrait Gallery)

Opposite page: Thomas Wentworth (1672-1739), third Earl of Strafford. A diplomat who fought with the Duke of Marlborough, he married Anne Johnson, daughter and heiress of Sir Henry Johnson who was Member of Parliament for Aldeburgh. Despite her letters to him describing 'pheasants, partridges and hares in vast quantity' he rarely visited his country estate in Suffolk. Oil on canvas, 312 x 224.5cm (© Crown copyright: UK Government Art Collection)

Certain names hang over Aldeburgh from generation to generation. One of these is the grandly-named Leveson Vernon Strafford Wentworth who lived much of his life in self-imposed darkness.

Leveson Vernon Wentworth's family had lived in Aldeburgh since long before 1500 when his mother's family name of Johnson first appears in the borough archive. She was Henrietta Johnson and her ancestor Francis Johnson built ships in Slaughden at the time of the Armada. A product of many generations of local nobility, Leveson Vernon Wentworth had Aldeburgh and the sea in his bones.

The Wentworths, Leveson's father's family, came to Aldeburgh in 1717, when Thomas Wentworth, third Earl of Strafford, married Anne Johnson, the heiress, and daughter of Sir Henry Johnson MP and then owner of the manor of Aldeburgh.

Thomas Wentworth's grandfather, the first Earl of Strafford, was a shrewd and close adviser to King Charles I. However, this Strafford was deserted by the King and executed in 1641 at the outset of the English Civil War by public demand. The outcry against him was because he had persuaded the Irish to join the King and take arms against the English Parliamentarians. He had become known as 'Black Tom Tyrant' and among his most notoriously damaging actions was the introduction of English protestant aristocracy into the ownership of much of the land of Catholic Ireland. The terrible effects of this initiative lasted many centuries.

His grandson, whose name was also Thomas Wentworth, fought with the Duke of Marlborough and has gone down in history as a blundering 'diplomat' who died of drink, but in Suffolk he was a prominent landowner and the family were house-builders in Aldeburgh, which is why the name is well-known. Strafford House still stands on Crag Path. The Wentworth family built and lived in Blackheath House and they designed and occupied the original house at Aldeburgh Lodge which was called Marine Villa. They also lived in Friston Hall. The manorial lands of Aldeburgh that he administered lie to the west of the town along the river front and north to Aldringham. The town map still has Wentworth Street and, of course, the Wentworth Hotel at the north end facing the sea.

Anne Johnson Wentworth wrote to her alcoholic husband, trying to persuade him to come to Aldeburgh in May 1729: 'I cannot imagine, my dear, why you do not like this place, for I think at this time it is the garden of the world; pheasants, partridges and hares are in vast quantity; wildfowl is plenty; all sorts of fish we have for nothing; our servants are almost cloyed with lobsters and soles.'

Leveson Vernon Wentworth, her grandson, was her daughter's third child. He was, by the end of his life, very eccentric. One of his responsibilities as lord of the manor was to pay and care for the vicar and the church. It was he who purchased and placed the current clock on the church. When the vicarage was being rebuilt in 1875 he loaned Marine Villa to the vicar's family, and many years later Georgina Thompson, the vicar's wife, wrote:

> 'It was a weird house, built by an eccentric bachelor who thought that if he went to bed for the hours of daylight and lived and moved and had his being at night, he would live the longer. The dining room and kitchens were underground so that he was sure of having his breakfast and his morning supper by lamplight, and he did not venture out of doors except during the hours of darkness. He kept a yacht and went out on the sea at night. He would call on his friends at 10pm and if they offered him refreshment he declined, saying it was too soon after his breakfast.'

> 'The basement was also occupied by toads and rats, of which the children became enamoured, but the ground floor was a very large room running the whole length of the house, but was divided into three by folding doors. With strange contradiction it had great windows reaching from the floor to the ceiling, which gave an uninterrupted view of the sea. The bedroom floors sloped towards little half moon shaped windows which also looked over the water.'

There is another description of the inside of Marine Villa which describes that same large room as 'a splendid reception room and two small octagonal rooms at each end and the doors were all concealed by being made to open out of the corners of the rooms, each door being shaped to shut into the corner.' Nor was this all, the walls were panelled and the panels opened with springs and shutter cases which could be opened only by those who knew their secret. In a passage behind the salon was a flagstone that could be lifted up to show a wooden stairway which led to a complete suite of rooms below ground.

The other great house of Leveson Vernon Wentworth is on the north bank of the river Alde at Hazelwood outside Aldeburgh. Known as Blackheath House, it can only be seen half-hidden by trees from the river and few people know of it. It remained in the Wentworth family until 1992 when the house was sold. Today, Hazelwood is a forgotten

settlement outside Aldeburgh – lost in the trees and the pine woods without road or path or river jetty: a place for wildlife only.

Few families have made more impression on the Aldeburgh that is to be seen today than the Garretts. From their initiative came the Jubilee Hall, the Brudenell Hotel, most of the buildings in the upper part of the town and, of course, the Maltings at Snape, home to the famous concert hall and Aldeburgh Festival. Their influence stretches far beyond the town to hospitals and particularly to the emancipation of women. It is a fascinating story.

The Garrett family were gunsmiths at the time of the Armada, supplying weapons to ships built in Aldeburgh. For several hundred years they were known as 'edge tool makers' which means the manufacture of harvesting tools for farmers. The great iron works at Leiston were started by the great-grandson of the original Richard Garrett in 1778 when he was twenty-one and he took over the use of an existing forge at the same place. In the same year he married the daughter of Henry Newson who lived in Leiston and in 1779 they had a son who became the fifth Richard Garrett.

When he was only sixteen, the young Richard Garrett married Sarah Balls, daughter of the Hethersett iron worker John Balls, who was the inventor of an improved threshing machine. Richard and Sarah had three sons: Richard, Balls and Newson. It was the rivalry between two of the three brothers which added so much to the story of Aldeburgh. They were the sixth Richard Garrett and his brother Newson, the first and third sons, (the middle son was called Balls after his mother). It is also a notable feature of the Garrett men that the women they chose to marry were strong and influential.

Brudenell Hotel in 1903. Newson Garrett designed and built a number of rows of houses in the town, of which Brudenell Terrace is considered his masterpiece. (Francis Frith Collection)

When he was twenty one, Richard Garrett the sixth, already financial manager of his father's business, married Elizabeth Dunnell, an innkeeper's daughter from London who had been born further up the Suffolk coast in Dunwich. At the wedding, Richard's sixteen-year-old brother Newson became infatuated with Elizabeth's younger sister, Louisa. It was to have momentous consequences for the fortunes of the family and for Aldeburgh.

Newson persuaded his parents to allow him to leave home and go to stay with the Dunnell family at their inn, which still exists and is called *The Beehive*, in Marylebone. He did not join the Garrett family business and chose, instead, to work for Mr Dunnell and learn the trade of pawnbroking.

Newson Garrett (1812–93). In the words of the Aldeburgh historian H. P. Clodd, Garrett was 'an outstanding personality in the affairs of Aldeburgh, possessed of great force of character and from small beginnings created great business interests'. The distribution centre he designed and built at Snape Maltings for barley, coal and other goods is now the world-famous concert venue, and his pioneering spirit continued through the work of several of his children, namely Elizabeth, Millicent, and Agnes, who each achieved success in their relative fields of medicine, women's suffrage, and architecture.
(Mary Evans Picture Library)

Around 1818 Newson Garrett's elder brother Richard became the overall manager of Leiston iron works. Richard was just twenty-three when his father died and bequeathed him the ownership of the entire industry and almost all his property. In stark contrast, Newson was given very little in his father's will, nor was his other brother, Balls.

For four years Newson Garrett worked for Mr Dunnell in the east end of London and then in his own pawn shop on Longacre in Covent Garden. When he was twenty-one he requested permission to marry Louisa and the wedding was held in the following year. Within seven years Newson and Louisa Garrett had five children, four of whom survived: Millicent, Elizabeth, Newson and Edmund.

However, after eight years in London, Newson Garrett was frustrated with his lack of progress. He and Louisa were living in Whitechapel and were driven by the needs of a growing family. They took a Suffolk sailing ship on its return journey from Canary Wharf, and with all their furniture and four small children, they sailed home to Aldeburgh and purchased an old house called Uplands on the high ground near to the church, where it can still be seen today. Louisa was well aware from her childhood of the stories of the many beachfront houses of Dunwich which had been lost to the sea, and she insisted that the family home was in a safe location. Uplands was also the house in which George Crabbe had earlier trained to be an apothecary.

Newson Garrett came to Aldeburgh with some money he had earned from his shop in London and some given to him by Louisa's father. He used his savings to purchase the business of an old corn and coal merchant near the Alde road bridge at Snape called Osborne and Fennell. The business consisted of a fleet of sailing barges or 'Hoys' and the mercantile dealing that went with the purchase and sale of goods, primarily corn, which was shipped from the site at Snape Bridge to Slaughden and thence to London. On their return journey the barges brought coal for Framlingham and the other local villages.

When Newson took over the business he started to buy barley instead of corn. He knew many of the London brewers through his connections with his father-in-law's inn, and he realised that they needed good barley to make their beer. It was a simple and brilliant idea, and Newson made a fortune very quickly. The market in London for Suffolk barley and malt was huge. Demand for ale was high in the inns and taverns of the most prosperous city in the world.

From the beginning Newson Garrett was driven by a desire to outdo his older brother in Leiston. As his trading business became profitable he embarked on building the beautiful and cleverly designed complex on the Alde which is called Snape Maltings. The plan of the place was centred around a turntable from which trolleys were received through the main archway, loaded up and then turned around to be sent to the river to unload their cargo onto the waiting ships on the quay.

The quay was the loading point for malt to go to
London, until it was replaced by the railway line.
Rob Barnes, Snape Maltings, etching and aquatint.
Reproduced by kind permission of the artist.

Elizabeth Garrett (1836-1917) as a young woman. She was the second daughter of Newson and Louisa Garrett and was the first woman to qualify in medicine (1865); the first woman to found a hospital (1866); the first woman dean of a medical school (1883) and for some years the only woman member of the British Medical Association, to which she was admitted in 1873. In later life she became the first female mayor in Britain when she took up the office in Aldeburgh in 1908.
(Royal London Hospital Archives and the Garrett family)

When the buildings at Snape Maltings were marked out, the tramlines were placed first and cemented into the ground as one would do in a pithead and the carts were horse-drawn. The whole operation was an advanced distribution centre linking farms to storage to malting to ships. Newson Garrett was the architect. It is even said that the long front of the building is not straight because he drew it out by hand on the ground and the bricklayers followed his line.

As his wealth grew, Newson Garrett acquired the whole of the land on top of the high ground of Aldeburgh to the south of Uplands. He built Alde House and eventually several other large houses for members of his family along Park Road, including what is now the hospital. The old gates which stand on either end of Park Road mark the ends of the Garrett estate which also had a brick wall around much of it. The bricks come from the Aldeburgh brickworks which Newson Garrett developed for his work at Snape and in Aldeburgh. He also bought the land which had previously been the fortress on the sea front and he built a row of houses that he called Brudenell Terrace, named out of admiration for Brudenell, Lord Cardigan, who was a distant relative and who led the Charge of the Light Brigade in the Crimea. Most of that row has now become the Brudenell Hotel.

Garrett was an enthusiast for the Crimean War and encouraged the Aldeburgh fishermen to join the navy. He had a much closer natural affinity with the beach boatmen than with the burgesses or the high society house owners. When the new lifeboat was caught in a terrible storm, Garrett took the helm of his own boat with one of his own children, and led a rescue. Louisa, it is said, stood vigil on the beach, praying for them both.

There was even a plan, supported by Newson Garrett, to cut through the wall at Slaughden so that the Alde would once again flow straight into the sea. Such a scheme had to be proposed to Parliament and it was rejected. For Garrett the advantage of not having to send his ships south of Orford in order to meet the sea was obvious. The enterprise would have returned the landscape to that of Roman times. Who knows whether it was the right thing to do? Perhaps Slaughden and its dock would have survived and still stand. The Three Mariners would be a popular place from which to watch the boats on the river and in the estuary. Instead Garrett turned to the new railway system to reduce the time and cost of transportation.

In contrast to the grime and filth of the foundry in Leiston which had made his brother so famous locally, Newson Garrett enjoyed an outdoor life of ships and the sea, riding from Aldeburgh to Snape along the old sailor's path, and sailing down the Alde. His family prospered and his children were clever and content. In *Sophia's Son* he was described by the vicar's wife, as 'tall, fair haired and dashing' but the best indicators of his character lie in his dealing with his daughter Elizabeth. Newson was not aristocratic, like the Crespigny family of Aldeburgh or the groups that played card games in the Thellusson

Garrett & Sons double-cylinder steam ploughing engine and tackle. Line engraving, 1862. (Science Museum/Science & Society Photo Library)

Casino. He was 'new money' in a way that his brother was not. Richard was an industrial agriculturalist: Newson was an astute dealer in commodities who could spot a new business opportunity and rapidly act on it. There was a touch of the righteous evangelism about him, too. As his wealth grew, he believed above all in himself and his own judgement, and his instinct was that his children should have faith in themselves, in the same way.

In Aldeburgh the Garrett children were taught by a governess, but Louisa was firm in her view that the girls should have a proper education and not just be brought up to become rich wives and housekeepers. This was rare, but it was not unique. There were many Victorian families in which the daughters were very well educated: Florence Nightingale, for example, spoke several languages, was highly competent in science and politics and was an excellent mathematician and statistician. The problem was that this academic capability in young ladies was usually frustratingly wasted, or had to be channelled through the influence of men. The Garrett girls were sent to a boarding school in Greenwich at which their father insisted to the school authorities that, amongst other matters, they should be allowed to have hot baths.

Boarding school gave the Garrett girls an introduction to other rich families around the country and a taste for the benefits of country house living. Elizabeth, the younger daughter, belonged to a set of wealthy and vivacious young ladies with shared ideas and a common belief that women should be allowed to play their role in society. The group was particularly impressed by an American woman called Elizabeth Blackwell. At a time when the idea that a woman should be a doctor was unthinkable in England, Dr Blackwell had paid her own way through New York medical school to become qualified and started a practice in the slums of Manhattan. To Elizabeth Garrett and her friends, Dr Blackwell was a heroine.

When Elizabeth Blackwell visited London after the Crimean War to pay her respects to Florence Nightingale, she held court in an apartment in Fitzrovia in London. Elizabeth Garrett travelled to meet her and the encounter clarified her determination to become a doctor. She was not the first woman to want to do this: others before her had tried to persuade the male surgical and medical establishments but none had ever succeeded in undertaking the seven-year programme of training that was required.

Elizabeth Garrett researched the matter and broke the news to her parents just after her twenty-fourth birthday. Mrs Garrett was appalled by the idea and could hardly speak in response. Newson Garrett supported his wife and told Elizabeth that he found Dr Blackwell to be distasteful. The matter, he said, was not even to be considered.

But Elizabeth was not to be dissuaded. She mounted a campaign to persuade her father and told him that he had no experience of that which he was dismissing. After only a week of her persuasive arguing, Newson changed his view completely and he told his daughter that he would support her in every way that he could. He went to Harley Street with her, and his encounter with the bigoted male medical establishment only strengthened his resolve to support her. In due course Elizabeth Garrett - with the robust support of her father - became the first woman doctor in England. This episode was entirely in character for both of them, in their determination and focus, even to the extent of disregarding the reservations of Elizabeth's mother, Louisa Garrett. Elizabeth's achievement changed the role of women in medicine forever. Newson's earlier reproach to the greybeards of Harley Street that 'I would rather have a properly trained woman doctor look after my wife and my daughters than a male doctor' had come to pass.

Whilst Elizabeth Garrett was training to become a doctor and thereby making a path for other women to follow, her sister Millicent was blazing her own trail in the radical movement to give women the vote. Throughout the nineteenth century there was continuous pressure to reform politics and advance the democratic right to vote to more than just a privileged few.

Aldeburgh was one of the seats of Parliament identified in 1834 as a 'rotten borough', which meant that the two MP's from Aldeburgh were not rightly elected, they represented only a few people and their seat had been bought rather than earned by fair election. Millicent Garrett, like her sister, became part of a group of young women who sought routes to change society, in this case to persuade influential members of parliament that reform not only meant disposing of unworthy membership of parliament, but it also meant giving the franchise to them and women like them.

After Newson Garrett had won the fight for Elizabeth to enter medical school, he returned to Aldeburgh and publicly declared himself to have become a Liberal. For a country gentleman of his standing – especially to his Tory brother Richard in Leiston –

Millicent Garrett (1847-1929) the fifth daughter and seventh child of Newson and Louisa Garrett. A prominent suffragist, she became president of the National Union of Women's Suffrage Societies. She was made a Dame of the British Empire in 1929, the year she died.
(Mary Evans Picture Library)

this was an appalling declaration of political misjudgement. His parents, Richard and Sarah, and his brother and sister-in-law responded by declaring their shock. In contrast, Millicent found that her father's stand strengthened her own fervour and her political position. Once again, Newson had shown himself to be an independent thinker who was well-matched by the intellect and strength of his daughters.

Reading the historical accounts of the family, there is also no doubt that the bond that held the the family unit together was created by Louisa, Garrett's wife. She was small and alongside him must have been physically overshadowed, but there is no doubt of his devotion and even obedience to her moods and mind.

Elizabeth married a ship owner called Skelton Anderson who in due course became mayor of Aldeburgh. They lived in a house in Park Road, and their stable was across the road to the south of the hospital, and when Skelton died Elizabeth turned it into her own home.

Millicent married Henry Fawcett, a leading Liberal politician. Fawcett was blind, but achieved prominence as a Minister under William Gladstone. In 1880 he was appointed Postmaster General, and was responsible for a number of innovations including the Post Office savings stamp and the postal order.

READ
OUR
PAPER
VOTES
FOR
WOMEN
VOTES FOR WOMEN
1D
WEEKLY
H.M. Dallas.

It is not obvious nowadays that in the later years of the nineteenth century Aldeburgh was a hotbed of political ideas and discussion. The relatives and friends of the Garrett family regularly assembled to debate issues at the centre of late-Victorian politics. Nevertheless, despite their national and international prominence, the children of Newson Garrett never lost their attachment to, or affection for, their town. They regarded its care as part of their responsibility.

Millicent was a co-founder of Newnham Ladies College at Cambridge in 1871 but she turned down an offer of being the Mistress of Girton College. Instead she became president of the National Union of Women's Suffrage Societies, which originally set out to achieve their aims by peaceful means. While Millicent clearly admired Emmeline Pankhurst, she did not agree with the violent actions of her group, the Women's Social and Political Union, who had split away from the NUWSS. In 1905 when the Liberals won the general election, the leaders of both groups were convinced that their long campaign would at last be successful. However in 1908 Herbert Asquith became leader of the Liberal party and it became clear to them both that he was not going to endorse the enfranchisement of women. So Millicent joined forces with Pankhurst and they moved their support from the Liberal to the Labour party. Eventually this change brought them success and it also proved one of the major reasons for the decline of the Liberals and the growth of Labour as a party of power in the 1920s.

When Skelton Anderson died, his widow Dr Elizabeth Garrett Anderson was elected Mayor of Aldeburgh, and so became the first woman mayor in England. She undertook the role with her customary vigour and installed electric lights in the streets of the town among many other major improvements. She served for two terms and insisted, at last, on the removal of the remains of the unsightly old pier; she installed public toilets; purchased electric pumps for the town water and built the first boat pond which was next to Slaughden Quay. She also oversaw the construction of a drainage system which keeps the town streets from flooding.

It is astonishing how much the town and the whole country, owes to the Garrett family, and how much the appearance and character of Aldeburgh derives from their energy and labour.

Shell-making during World War I at the station works of the Garrett factory in Leiston. Note that all of the workers are women.
Private collection, reproduced by kind permission of Michael Walters.

Workers at the main entrance to the Garrett factory. The factory was divided into two sections: the top factory was next to the old railway station, and the bottom factory (seen here) near the Post Office Square.
Private collection, reproduced by kind permission of Michael Walters.

CHAPTER 11:
DEFENCE AND WAR

Along the coast, on the beach at Felixstowe there is a visitor information point, which contains an engraved map, looking eastwards out to sea. It reminds the visitor of the defensive position of this area of the coast in relation to the countries of Europe, Asia and Scandinavia. Thousands of years ago, tidal waves brought the separation of the land masses of Britain and Europe, and ever since that time, the east coast formed and played a major part in the defence of the island from powerful overseas nations.

At various times Romans, Danes, Saxons, Dutch, Russians, Germans, Dunkirkers, French and Spanish forces have attempted to land on or to threaten this coastline. Aldeburgh has often found itself in a key defensive position and its people in the front line of immediate military activity.

So far as one can tell, the method used by all these invading forces was to move into the river estuaries along the east coast and then to find a point where it was practical to ford the river with a causeway or a bridge. These places then became important strategic positions as the firm beaches around the river estuary upon which craft could be hauled. Therefore the defending communities would have been concerned to make sure such strongholds were not taken and occupied. This helps to explain why both Aldeburgh and Snape became continuously inhabited communities, important because of their ability to defend against repeated attacks.

The first raids by foreign invaders were intended for the theft of gold and other treasure: the object was to return home with wealth. These sailors would not have travelled further than a few miles from an estuary or port; if they found a building to plunder there was no need to go further. Raids of this kind went on profitably for years after the Roman army left. By 600 AD, after repeated attacks, the lands of East Anglia had become Anglo-Saxon but these settlers were in turn invaded by the Viking Danes who began the process again.

We do not know what it was like to live in a town at the head of a river estuary into which the Saxon boats entered, but it must have been more terrifying than any later age was to experience. Imagine Aldeburgh beach and the Alde estuary experiencing raids every night, year after year, until no possession was left and no family was safe from violent harassment. There is nothing of the Roman villa at Barber's Point or any other construction and almost no remnant of earlier years, unless it is deeply buried and yet to be discovered.

Shortly after the time of the Second Crusade it was possible to take a boat up the river Alde as far upstream as Framlingham. Framlingham Castle was originally built by the

166

Henry Bright, Orford Castle, 1856, oil on canvas, 104.8 x 168.7cm. (Norwich Castle Museum and Art Gallery)

Saxon king Raedwald but the Normans gave it to Hugh Bigod, Earl of Norfolk, a powerful and domineering character who bullied the descendants of William the Conqueror in the way he controlled the region. Bigod had made his money from the sale of local wool and he had little concern for anything other than his own chests of gold. In fact he did the most treacherous thing: he made an alliance with the Flemish and the Dunkirkers and arranged for them to invade and fight with him against the King in order to protect his interests. All the coastal towns were forced to arm themselves against these attacks. King Edward built Orford Castle in 1165 in order to prevent an invasion but the great defence, of which only the keep tower still stands, was a failure because the landing boats simply avoided it and came ashore further along the coast. Henry II eventually surrounded Framlingham but Hugh Bigod avoided defeat by agreeing to join the King in the Third Crusade to the Holy Land. The Bigods lost none of their power in this encounter and they remained a force of local tyranny. Roger Bigod (second son of Hugh) was one of those who brought King John to Runnymede to make him sign the Magna Carta.

For the next 500 years, the story of the Aldeburgh coastline was of sea battles, raids, pirates, and foreign incursions of painful constancy. Whether the fight was for fish or for the defence of the country, it must have always been a source of distress for the residents of the town. Aldeburgh had always been a naval and military town, until the last years of the twentieth century when the end of the Cold War with the Soviet Union allowed the air defences to be relaxed. Orford Ness is still littered with sophisticated and sometimes secret defensive technology.

167

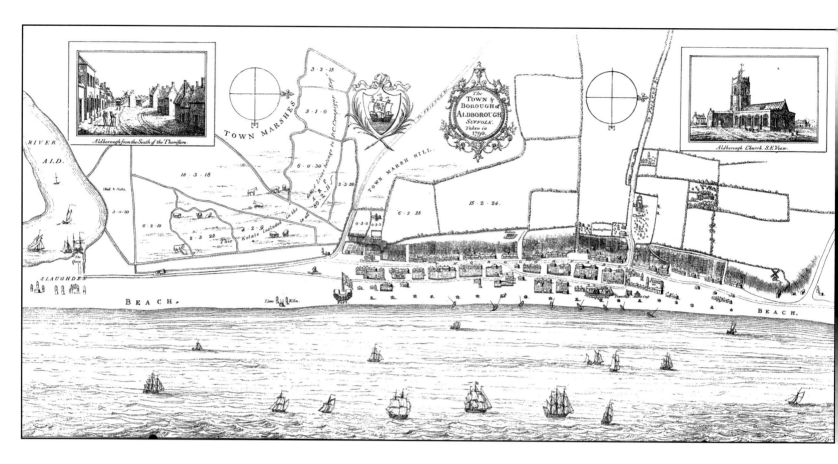

A map of Aldeburgh in 1740.
(Ipswich Record Office)

In 1626 the Duke of Buckingham, who was then Lord High Admiral, assessed Aldeburgh to be at high risk of invasion and declared that 10,000 men might land and reach the town without resistance.

Three half-moon-shaped fortresses were built at Buckingham's command on the beach, and a number more on the cliff top. There was one positioned on the beach in front of the current Brudenell Hotel. Its arsenal and powder house were where the hotel car park is now. This is the origin of the name 'Fort Green'. Despite these defences, local fishermen were afraid to go out and the ability of the fishing fleet to feed the residents declined. Their fears were well-founded: in 1630, the French captured a whole flotilla of Aldeburgh fishing boats and took them to France. There were continual sea battles and the government called on the dockyards in the town to supply more fighting ships and crews for them. It was this demand for naval construction that made several local families rich.

Stories of Britain in the First World War concentrate on the battlefields of Flanders and northern France but often neglect to tell of what happened in England. As early as December 1914, within three months of the war starting, the German navy launched a bombardment of shells on towns along the east coast.

Aldeburgh was the home of one of the first aerodromes constructed along the east coast as the battle in the air became part of the fighting strategy. An airstrip was constructed to the west of the golf course at Grange Farm. The route to it lies off the road to Saxmundham. The role of the airmen at the Aldeburgh airfield was to track and shoot down German Zeppelin airships that were being used to bomb English cities.

There was one Zeppelin hit over Theberton when sixteen members of a German crew died having been struck by fire from a local fighter plane in June 1917. The remains of the structure of the balloon are still on display in the church.

Towards the end of the war the protection of supply shipping dominated the war agenda, so the air station at Aldeburgh was turned into a training school for reconnaissance over the sea. The crews were taught how to spot and bomb German submarines from the air. Building work on the aerodrome required a railway line to be built from Grange Farm down to the Alde at Barber's Point, exactly where the Romans had previously used the quay to land their own military equipment. The rail track followed the main road and then cut down across what is now the southern section of the golf course to the river.

The history of the aerodrome, of which little remains, is touched with sadness. Shortly after the end of the war, two planes collided in an exercise over Thorpeness. Three young airmen who had survived the war died in the incident and are buried in the churchyard. The people of Aldeburgh have always travelled in their boats to distant countries; that is their inheritance. But in the Great War of 1914-18, men (and some women), mostly very young, travelled further than many of their ancestors, and sadly many of them did not return. The war memorial which was constructed outside the Moot Hall after that war and unveiled in January 1921 records the names of those who died. There is no more telling description of the town and its residents than the stories which lie behind these details and what they reveal. The sheer number of people and of the countries they fought in demonstrates the magnitude of that war. The list forms a picture not only of those who are honoured but of the parents and families they left behind. For each of these names there are class-mates, school friends and neighbours or fellow members of a club, group or team. Descendants of many of those who gave their lives still live here or have close connections with the town.

The statistics are merciless. At the beginning of the war the population of the town was about 2,300 people. Eighty-four people who died are commemorated on the war memorial from seventy families. Sixteen were in the navy, two men recorded were in the Air Force and one in the Flying Corps and the remaining sixty-five were in the army. Of those whose age is known, seventeen were twenty-one-years-old or less. Half of the named people died in France or Flanders. Christine Jay, a nurse, is the only woman whose name appears.

From the point of view of one small town of no particular political or geographical significance related to the causes of the conflict, the devastation and tragedy of the Great War was immense. The loss to parents and families was and is unimaginable in its cruelty.

When World War II broke out in 1939 the sea lanes off the Aldeburgh shore were immediately laid with mines, and within only a few days the German tanker SS *Magdapur*

Thomas Churchyard, Fort Green, Aldeburgh, watercolour, 29 x 19cm. (Private collection)

sank off the beach. Its seventy-four crew members were rescued in the first of many wartime launches of the town lifeboat.

The British government planned on the basis that there was going to be a German invasion of East Anglia by sea and by airborne troops. The assumption was that the enemy would aim their first attacks on one or more towns in which it would be possible to land soldiers and equipment. The English planned to retaliate by concentrating their efforts on the defeat of the accompanying airborne invasion, as this would cause the whole assault to fail. For this reason Reserve Territorial Army divisions were placed along the whole east coast ready to be deployed to wherever the landings took place. This strategy was called the Julius Caesar Plan. As before in the seventeenth century, Aldeburgh was regarded as a place vulnerable to invasion because an army could land on the town beach and take hold, while the marshes to the north and the river to the south would make it difficult to counter-attack by land. This was exactly the same argument Buckingham had used in 1626 to build fortress positions on the sea front. The difference in 1939 was the presence of air defence, but no one knew at that point whether the RAF would hold out against the Luftwaffe: one had to face the possibility that it might not.

At Aldeburgh there was a line drawn from the north bank of the river, across the golf course to Leiston and on to Westleton and Blythburgh. The order was that the sector, which was defended by 2/4th Essex Battalion, would be held as a line, and there would be no withdrawal from it. In addition, defensive positions were set up from the Martello Tower along the beach north as far as Minsmere. The beach guns included Howitzers and machine-gun positions. The road from Aldeburgh to Saxmundham would be a route for escaping refugees and the order was that in the event of movement of civilians west along that road, no vehicle or telephone line would be left behind that could be useful to the enemy. In 1940 the local battalions were strengthened in the same positions by regiments from Lancashire.

In May 1940 the government formed the Local Defence Volunteers to make use of any man between seventeen and sixty-five who was not on active service in the main armed forces. The response to this, particularly in rural areas, was overwhelming, and local police stations were inundated with volunteers. At the time there had been several invasion warnings – and it was in the summer of 1940 that Winston Churchill, who had just become prime minister, made his famous call for England to 'fight on the beaches… and we shall never surrender', which rang especially true in coastal areas of the south and east of the country. This speech was a profound inspiration to those who were guarding the sea front against an invasion. The history of the local regiment records that while the volunteer soldiers had little but their bare hands with which to fight, 'we would have annihilated the hated Nazis somehow'.

It is absolutely to be expected of the town that an official report on morale in the area also said:

> Considering that the town is one of the quietest and dullest places in Britain the degree of depression and irritation in Aldeburgh is not remarkably high. Extremely unpleasant things are said about local leaders.

In June 1940, two six-inch naval guns were mounted at the south end of the town on the site of the old washhouse, where the coastguard station now stands. Reade's the builders constructed two steel frames to carry the great weapons. This was also the original site of the Elizabethan fort which had exactly the same purpose of defending the town and the coastline four hundred years before. In addition to these two guns, a whole set of decoy gun positions were built along the road between Aldeburgh and Thorpeness.

Alan Bridges, The Martello Tower, watercolour. Reproduced by kind permission of the artist.

171

Jules George, What Became of Marengo? (Martello
Tower, Aldeburgh), 2008, oil on canvas, 92 x 76cm.
Reproduced by kind permission of the artist.

The beach was laid with mines, one of which caused a fatal accident at Thorpeness. Gun carriages were mounted on the railway line and moved up and down the coast from Saxmundham to Ipswich, ready to be used in the event of attack. Later the concrete bunkers that are still part of the local landscape were constructed by the Royal Engineers. There are 175 of these spread along the coastline.

The Aldeburgh economy before 1939 depended upon tourism and fishing, but as the hostilities started, both of these became impossible to continue. It was a depressing time to endure. Even the golf club closed down, and the military activity on the beach made the townspeople wonder if the shingle would ever be restored to its former beauty. Nonetheless, the people who stayed were determined and proud.

The land from Iken to Sudbourne was completely evacuated and became part of a military training zone. Everybody was forced to move from their homes and they were forbidden to return until peacetime. This was clearly very hard for many people who had hardly moved out of the area in their lives. The land, which had been a battleground in Roman times, was said to resemble the terrain of Flanders and was needed to acclimatize the army and to test its equipment, particularly the new kinds of tanks that were being developed. Special devices were being engineered for adapting tanks as mine clearers and track layers were tested in the Iken flats; they later became a very important part of the equipment used for the invasion of Europe.

The windmill was used as the observation point for the World War Two emergency coastal battery at Aldeburgh, and the small square building attached to it was added during the war as the range finder post. The concrete blocks in the foreground were placed to prevent German tanks from coming inland from the beach. Photograph by Dave Thurlow, reproduced by kind permission of the photographer.

In August 1940 one of the most mysterious events of wartime England occurred at Aldeburgh and there still is no definitive explanation of just what happened. A theory exists that an actual German invasion took place. The Allied defence forces were ready, and covered the sea in oil which was then torched. All the landing craft were destroyed just off Shingle Street, and for some days afterwards the tarred corpses of German soldiers were washed ashore and then hidden. Nobody wanted to reveal how the attack had been countered in case the same method was used against the Allied forces in the future.

There are other explanations of the explosions and firestorms of that night, including the rather less exciting one that the bomb designer Barnes Wallace accidentally destroyed the Lifeboat Inn at Shingle Street, but that might have happened on any one of a number of days when he was working. Barnes Wallace was the scientist made famous for his invention of the bouncing bombs used in the raids on German dams. What is certain is that from many miles around, there were reports of a major and extended battle during one night. The government said nothing at the time and have never disclosed what really happened. One has to suppose that they did not want to reveal the defensive methods that were used. At the time it was vital that the German High Command did not copy what they did, and since then it has become regarded as an episode of which no one can speak without horror.

For the next month the whole of the coast was on constant alert. On the evening of 7 September all the forces in the area were given the code 'Cromwell' which was the alert to prepare for an invasion at dawn the next morning. This followed RAF reconnaissance which had reported exceptional levels of enemy craft movement in the ports of continental Europe facing East Anglia. The Cromwell order included instructions to destroy bridges and roads in order to prevent the advance of the German army when it had landed.

The entire coast was on silent watch all that night in order to hear the sounds of ships approaching. But nothing happened; mercifully the warning turned out to be a false alarm.

This is all that now remains of the No 1 gun emplacement which still had a roof until the mid-1990s. Not much else is left of the World War II defences at Aldeburgh, but there are some small trenches and pill boxes to the north west at North Warren, and ditches widened as anti-tank traps are still visible on Church Farm marches to the north of the town.
Photograph by Dave Thurlow, reproduced by kind permission of the photographer.

Martin Laurance, Pale Sun, Orford Ness, 2012,
34 x 31cm, mixed media on paper (indian ink,
acrylic ink, collage, acrylic paint, watercolour).
Reproduced by kind permission of the artist.

176

Martin Laurance, Houses at Shingle Street II, 2011, 52 x 57cm, mixed media on paper (indian ink, acrylic ink, collage, acrylic paint, watercolour). Reproduced by kind permission of the artist.

Aldeburgh was first bombed in October 1940 when the new Catholic church lost its tower. Over 165 other buildings in the town were damaged and six people were injured. Bombings and other attacks of various kinds took place over the next two years. In April 1941 a mine store in Oakley Square exploded and later that year on 6 October, several hundred mines on the beach between Aldeburgh and Thorpeness blew up in a spectacular display.

The most terrible night of bombing in Aldeburgh was from a single German plane on 15 December 1942. Firing a machine gun and dropping bombs along the High Street, it destroyed the old post office, the cottage hospital and several other buildings. Eleven people died and twenty-nine others were injured. The electricity and gas supplies to the town were cut. The damage was immense but the town had to cope with it for several years, as repairs could not be made until the war ended.

After the war ended in 1945 the area resumed its role as part of the defence of Britain against the threat of invaders from the Soviet Union. On the Suffolk coast, a number of mysterious secret military buildings appeared on Orford Ness. At this time the the key military alliance was with the Americans and particularly their Air Force. They used the radar station at Orford Ness to track the paths of aircraft, at long distance, with varying degress of success. One notorious military initiative was called Cobra Mist. This was an attempt to create radar waves that curved with the earth's surface so they could detect military activity in distant Siberia. After many years' development it failed expensively, having cost the Americans over $100,000,000.

The original military installation on Orford Ness was built during the First World War when it was used for testing prototype aircraft. At one time 600 people were stationed on the peninsula and over the years many of their activities were classified as Top Secret. In addition to the development of radar, the site was used as part of the testing for the original parachutes, for camouflage, for 'black boxes', for aircraft bomb aimers, for propeller blade machine-guns and for aerial reconnaissance photography. Some say that the Ness was involved in the construction of atomic bombs, though in what role has always been kept secret. Now the land has been reopened as a sanctuary for wildlife.

In wartime the military bases were a potent mixture for social scandal, especially as such a large proportion of the local young men were away overseas on active service. American airmen and local girls socialised at dances and other occasions, and many illicit love affairs ensued.

Alex Tomlinson, The Aldeburgh Flying Platform,10.5 x 15cm. Reproduced by kind permission of the artist.

USAF airbase Bentwaters. Photography by Mike Page, reproduced by kind permission of the photographer.

In 1948 the American Air Force arrived in strength at a camp near Woodbridge which became a temporary home for many thousand of US military personnel. The airfield at Butley had been used as a base in 1940 during the Battle of Britain. After the war it became known as Bentwaters and was given to the American Airforce for their permanent sole use in 1951. For forty years American airforce men and their families formed part of the community and the area was witness to the most advanced fighter aircraft in the world, flying over Aldeburgh and patrolling the North Sea.

The area around Aldeburgh has recorded a number of sightings of unexplained phenomena. There have been even more sinister flying objects than German Zeppelins. In 1917 a Mrs Whiteland, who lived at the corner of the Leiston Road by the railway station observed a hovering 'platform' which carried men who were making observations as it came flying slowly over the marshes towards her. As it came close to the railway, the flying object turned to the right and gently moved off in the direction of the church and the sea.

Some years afterwards Mrs Whiteland's son made a drawing of his mother's description which caused some interest among those who follow these matters. He also drew a map which shows where the sighting took place.

This was not the only time that such a strange unaccountable object was sighted. A similar silent moving platform with about 30 'occupants' was observed flying near the railway lines in West Hampstead, London, by Reverend Pitt Kethly in 1955.

One cannot speak of the USAF without telling the tale of the spacecraft that is said to have landed in Rendlesham forest in December 1980.

Alien spacecraft were apparently observed on land between the two USAF airbases at Woodbridge and Bentwaters both on the 26 and 28 of December and the matter became the subject of official inquiries both by the American Air Force and the British Ministry of Defence. The report written by Lieutenant Colonel Halt, the Deputy Base Commander, records a number of observations and pieces of evidence. The object first seen was hovering above the ground and was 'described as being metallic in appearance and triangular in shape, approximately two to three meters across the base and two meters high. It illuminated the entire forest with a white light.' Its arrival appeared to be accompanied by other space craft visible in the night sky.

Clearly spacecraft design, if this came from the same planet as the platform seen by Mrs Whitelands, had progressed in the sixty years between the two recorded sightings. The open elegant brass rail construction of the first had become a more weather-proof vehicle by the second.

Many theories have been put forward for these occurrences including the notion that the whole event was a hoax, but Lt Colonel Halt's eyewitness account is still on the file of both the American Air Force and The British Ministry of Defence. Among the hoax theorists was Kevin Conde, who was there on the night, but, twenty years later claimed publicly that he had invented the whole story as a Christmas holiday joke. If that were true he obviously fooled the gullible station commander. Or, alternatively, someone persuaded him to change his story after all those years.

Opposite page: The USAF report of the events of 27 December 1980, written by the Deputy Base Commander, Lieutenant Colonel Halt.

One is reminded of the incident of 1643 when meteorites landed in several parts of the earth around the same time, and that one of those also had a deep effect on Aldeburgh and its people.

DEPARTMENT OF THE AIR FORCE
HEADQUARTERS 81ST COMBAT SUPPORT GROUP (USAFE)
APO NEW YORK 09755

REPLY TO
ATTN OF: CD

13 Jan 81

SUBJECT: Unexplained Lights

TO: RAF/CC

1. Early in the morning of 27 Dec 80 (approximately 0300L), two USAF
security police patrolmen saw unusual lights outside the back gate at
RAF Woodbridge. Thinking an aircraft might have crashed or been forced
down, they called for permission to go outside the gate to investigate.
The on-duty flight chief responded and allowed three patrolmen to proceed on foot. The individuals reported seeing a strange glowing object
in the forest. The object was described as being metalic in appearance
and triangular in shape, approximately two to three meters across the
base and approximately two meters high. It illuminated the entire forest
with a white light. The object itself had a pulsing red light on top and
a bank(s) of blue lights underneath. The object was hovering or on legs.
As the patrolmen approached the object, it maneuvered through the trees
and disappeared. At this time the animals on a nearby farm went into a
frenzy. The object was briefly sighted approximately an hour later near
the back gate.

2. The next day, three depressions 1 1/2" deep and 7" in diameter were
found where the object had been sighted on the ground. The following
night (29 Dec 80) the area was checked for radiation. Beta/gamma readings
of 0.1 milliroentgens were recorded with peak readings in the three depressions and near the center of the triangle formed by the depressions.
A nearby tree had moderate (.05-.07) readings on the side of the tree
toward the depressions.

3. Later in the night a red sun-like light was seen through the trees.
It moved about and pulsed. At one point it appeared to throw off glowing
particles and then broke into five separate white objects and then disappeared. Immediately thereafter, three star-like objects were noticed
in the sky, two objects to the north and one to the south, all of which
were about 10° off the horizon. The objects moved rapidly in sharp angular
movements and displayed red, green and blue lights. The objects to the
north appeared to be elliptical through an 8-12 power lens. They then
turned to full circles. The objects to the north remained in the sky for
an hour or more. The object to the south was visible for two or three
hours and beamed down a stream of light from time to time. Numerous individuals, including the undersigned, witnessed the activities in paragraphs
2 and 3.

CHARLES I. HALT, Lt Col, USAF
Deputy Base Commander

CHAPTER 12:
SEA AND LIFE

Off the coast of Aldeburgh there are sandbanks and channels which need careful navigation. Many ships have foundered within sight of shore, and the wind and tide along the coast sometimes destroy them before sailors can be rescued.

Nothing in Aldeburgh is more arresting than the explosive sound of the Maroon alarm call that summons the lifeboat crew into action. Within moments of its detonation the road at the lifeboat station will be swarming with lifeboatmen hurrying from all over the town, and the beach will be filled with clanking chains and huge tractors readying the boat for launch. The operation has pride, purpose and history all fused into an oily determination to get both the large boat and its small companion into the sea as fast as humanly possible. Whether the cause be the foolish antics of an inexperienced yachtsman on a summer afternoon or the horror of a major disaster on the sandbanks out at sea in the cold of winter, the professionally-rehearsed fierce urgency is always the same. A crowd on the beach has always watched both the going out and the return of the boat. Not many of the holidaymakers know of the terrible accidents of the past, nor have they been told of the awful night in 1899 when the lifeboat itself was lost, but those memories linger in the pubs and homes of the families that still crew the lifeboat as they have for many hundreds of years.

The lifeboat is the real, honest soul of Aldeburgh. It is almost like a religious institution for the town. When it is called out by the coastguard, the volunteer crews arrive from every direction, one for launching and the other for manning the ship as it heads off to sea. Its smaller sister, the in-shore craft, also has its own teams. Local people come to watch the launch and wait for the return of the two boats. That has been the practice since the time of the first sail-driven lifeboat on the beach ready for emergency and that came with the foundation of the volunteer body: The Royal National Lifeboat Institution in 1851. If Queen Elizabeth II were visiting the town, she would not take precedence over the launch of the lifeboat to a ship in distress.

The Aldeburgh lifeboat station keeps a proud record of all the occasions upon which the call has been made. On its website it tells the stories of outstanding rescues and heroes who undertook them. The building which houses the boat and its mechanical gear is a tough four-square construction of Scandinavian appearance that looks as if it would withstand the mightiest arctic storm. On its forecourt is the rudder of the old *City of Winchester*, the boat that came into service in 1902. These old boats were designed by the lifeboatmen of the town and built to their own specification and requirements. These men put their lives at risk each time they set sail, and they knew the best way to stay afloat in the most violent storms. They were remarkably tough sailors, just as the crews

Elizabeth Morris, Fishers of Men, etching and aquatint, 60 x 42cm.
Reproduced by kind permission of the artist.

182

Jack Pead with two cod. He was cox of the Aldeburgh lifeboat from 1929 to 1938.

are today. There are a few great natural talents that are passed from one generation to the next, and the musicians and lifeboatmen of Aldeburgh represent two of the best.

The earliest permanent presence of a boat and crew of townspeople was in 1851. Newson Garrett most certainly played a part in the creation of a lifeboat station, but the name in the town most associated with the boats is that of the Cable family.

James Cable was born in 1851 and saw his father drowned attempting a lifeboat rescue in 1855. His account of the incident, written towards the end of his life, says: 'The crew of the lifeboat were all saved including the pilot Rodney Pallant, who was a great friend of my father. Just before he got to the vessel he saved Mr Newson Garrett. The crew of the ship got the line, but it broke and he was taken under the vessel and never seen again.'

There have been famous rescues and many lives have been saved by the lifeboat. In 1892 the King of Norway presented medals to the entire crew of the Aldeburgh lifeboat after they had gone to the rescue of the shipwrecked crew of Norwegian barque *The Larvik*. Royal Medal 2nd Class went to coxwsain James Cable, and Royal Medals 3rd Class to W. Mann, A. Mann, John Greene, Charles Ward, James Ward, George Ward, Thomas Ward, Robert Cattel, George Knights, John Butcher, Robert Butcher, Charles Thorpe, William Wigg, William Crisp, John Downing, Henry Pearce and Thomas Cable.

James Cable's life is astonishing. At the age of thirteen when he was working in the shipyard, the master of a shipping smack asked him to come as cabin boy on a journey. In his autobiography he recalled that he had to go and find his mother, who was at a wedding in the church. He said 'She cried and took on and said I was not to go to sea, but an old lady with her said "If the boy wants to go to sea, let him go" so my mother bought me some warm clothes and I was there on time for the boat when it left.'

James Cable at the helm of the Aldeburgh lifeboat. He was coxswain from 1888 to 1917 and in total his length of service to the lifeboat was well over fifty years.

James Cable in retirement. His medals are, left to right: Royal National medal and two bars, second and third service; Norwegian and Swedish medal for saving a crew of seventeen Norwegians wrecked in the Alde Bay; the Royal Humane Medal for life-saving.
(Photographs from *A Lifeboatman's Days* by James Cable, 1927)

He tells of long journeys to Scandinavia and then to the China Seas. Eventually he signed up in London on a boat bound for Australia and there he learned to shear sheep on the farm of a long-lost uncle. 'We sheared 10,000 sheep at our first station, 20,000 at the next and 80,000 at the next,' he says.

'I received letters from home asking me to return', he wrote, and after a long and adventurous journey: 'I found my mother staying at her sister's in Sidcup and they were very pleased to see me.' In 1878 he married Emily Dyer of Cowes. On the morning of his marriage he went fishing and upset his wife 'in her condition' even though he had sold the catch for £23. In 1880 he was made second coxswain of the Aldeburgh lifeboat

The lifeboat *The Aldeburgh*
with her crew circa 1880.
(Francis Frith collection)

and was owner of a number of bathing machines on the beach. In 1888 he was made first coxswain and recounts many rescues including the tragic loss of the town lifeboat in December 1899. Many generations of Cables have since manned the Aldeburgh lifeboat, including his fifteen-year-old great grandson, who in 1954 defied the age regulation of twenty-one to scramble aboard the lifeboat as it went to assist a ship that had run aground at Orford Ness. 'They'll never keep a Cable out of the lifeboat' said his mother when she heard about his exploits, and she was quite right: the latest generation of the family (another James) was appointed as mechanic of the Aldeburgh lifeboat station in 1998.

In the history of the town and of Suffolk there can be few sadder moments than the morning of Thursday 7 December 1899.

The Aldeburgh had been called out to a fishing boat caught on the sands offshore. It was a difficult launch because the wind was blowing from the south east directly on to the beach. James Cable had been ordered by the doctor not to go on the boat, as he was ill, and so his place was taken by Charles Ward.

It was only possible to get the boat into the water a short way and raise the sails, because of the force of the wind, so Ward steered the ship down the beach until it was level with the Brudenell Hotel. Then he attempted to drive the ship out into deeper water. At that moment three enormous waves struck the boat and overturned it. It was less

186

than 100 yards from the shore and was driven upside down onto the beach with six crewmen underneath. The remaining twelve were in the water.

The crowd on the beach, led by James Cable, tried to open the hull of the boat with axes and when that failed they attempted to turn it over with poles. It is said there were 200 people on the beach who tried desperately to rescue the men in the sea and those trapped under lifeboat. Cable wrote 'I got on to the bottom and tried to hack through it with an axe, but after the planks there were air cases and the decks to get through and I could not do it. We tried to lift the boat with long poles but it was not until the tide went down hours after that my men were able to crawl under boat and we knew that the six poor fellows must be dead. That was a very sad day for Aldeburgh and will never be forgotten.' All six men who were unable to escape from the heavy shell had indeed perished, and one other crew member died later from his injuries. There is a monument in the churchyard to those who died and a moving model built by the Burwood family in the Moot Hall to recall the incident.

The Aldeburgh lifeboat capsized on the beach in December 1899.The crowd of people on the shore desparately tried to turn the lifeboat over to rescue the men trapped underneath. Twelve men were thrown clear when the lifeboat capsized, but six were trapped. Attempts were made to hack through the hull but to no avail.
(From *Sophia's Son* by Dorothy Thompson, Terence Dalton Publishing, 1969)

Aldeburgh beach has been home to several forms of activity apart from fishing and the lifeboats. There is a history of smuggling on the beaches of Suffolk that remains fascinating, especially when the possibility remains of finding buried treasure.

In the 1700s the customs officers were a meagre defence against the organised gangs of smugglers operating on a large scale throughout East Anglia. In Parliament it was said that a young man could earn far more from smuggling, and have a much more interesting life, than if he were to labour on a farm. The origin of the trade was a high tax on desirable imports which included not only spirits and alcohol but also Indian tea which carried a duty of over 110%. The smugglers had good contacts in the ports of Holland and ran an import business which included distribution and shipment to London and sale in the markets there.

Nightly evasion of the customs men in their revenue cutters meant goods were often buried on the beach, or stored in local buildings, such as pubs, and were sometimes buried inland away from the shore. In the early 1900s several important finds of valuable smugglers' treasure were made when digging on the beach at Thorpeness. It is quite likely that there are still troves to be found on Leiston Heath, the fields at Snape, or in the woods of Blackheath which were left behind in haste and never recovered.

Most notorious of the smugglers were the Hadleigh gang who operated the whole coastline from Yarmouth to Ipswich. The detailed logistics of their operations would put a multinational conglomerate to shame. They even had their own military protection in order to defend themselves against the guardsmen, and up to 300 carts a night were used on different beaches to collect goods from prearranged shipments. The leader of the Hadleigh gang was John Harvey, who was caught and convicted, but evading justice to the last, Harvey escaped execution on a technicality of law and was sent to Australia.

Alan Bridges, The Customs House on the High Street, watercolour.
Reproduced by kind permission of the artist.

Margaret Catchpole was a Suffolk girl who fell in love with a smuggler, Will Laud. She was employed by the Cobbold family of brewers in Ipswich as a maid to their children and there is some evidence that she saved one of their boys from drowning. Her downfall came when she was convicted for stealing a horse from the Cobbold stable to ride to London and find her lover. Margaret was a superb horsewoman and was only caught because the horse was very recognisable. She was sentenced to hang, but because of her dignity in court, and, rather unusually, the special pleading from the Cobbolds, the sentence was commuted to seven years in Ipswich gaol. She became a model prisoner, and after a year she was given privileged duties in the prison laundry, where she used the prison sheets to escape over the wall to freedom. Disguised as a sailor, Margaret met Will Laud outside the prison and intended to elope with him to Holland but the couple were caught on the beach at Havergate Island. He was shot and killed in the struggle and she was captured and tried again for jail breaking. She escaped death a second time and was

sent as a convict to Australia where she became a midwife and a highly regarded member of the community. Ironically, she was made famous by Richard Cobbold, a member of the brewing family from whom she had stolen the horse. He penned a cautionary tale of a good woman who had 'fallen' because of her liaison with the wrong sort of man based on a romanticised version of Margaret's life which became a Victorian best seller.

There have always been fishermen who needed to live on the beach in makeshift housing and there have sometimes been townsfolk who regarded them as messy, dirty and an unpleasant blot on their beach. In some other Edwardian towns these beach dwellers would be called 'Egyptians' or travellers, but the Aldeburgh boatmen and their families had hardly moved for 3,000 years except to travel over the sea and there was an unspoken agreement that they had the right to stay there. However, by the 1890s the beach huts and makeshift shelters had spread too widely for the taste of the local gentry. Leveson Vernon Wentworth, lord of the manor, sent bailiffs and police to clear away them away. 'It is untidy' he said. The fishermen retaliated by taking Wentworth's solicitor hostage and threatened to throw him in the sea. For several days there was a dramatic and angry stand-off on the beach.

More police were sent for and events became violent. Fighting broke out with homemade weapons fashioned from fishing equipment on the one side, and truncheons made of lignum vitae on the other. But numbers were against the beach dwellers and they were evicted. Many homes were destroyed with fearsome ease. The wealthy - once again - carried the day.

Margaret Catchpole stealing a horse. The remarkable adventures of this Suffolk woman included the theft of John Cobbold's carriage horse, which she rode through the night to London, in order to sell it and give the money to her lover, Will Laud. Unfortunately for her the horse was a striking strawberry roan with cropped ears, and was easily recognised. She was caught and sent to Ipswich gaol, from where she escaped three years later, in 1800. Original watercolour by Richard Cobbold, reproduced by permission of the Cobbold Family History Trust.

Overleaf:
Thomas Churchyard (1798-1865), A Fisherman's Hut by the Sea, oil on board, mounted as a drawing, 14 x 21.5cm. (Ashmolean Museum Oxford)

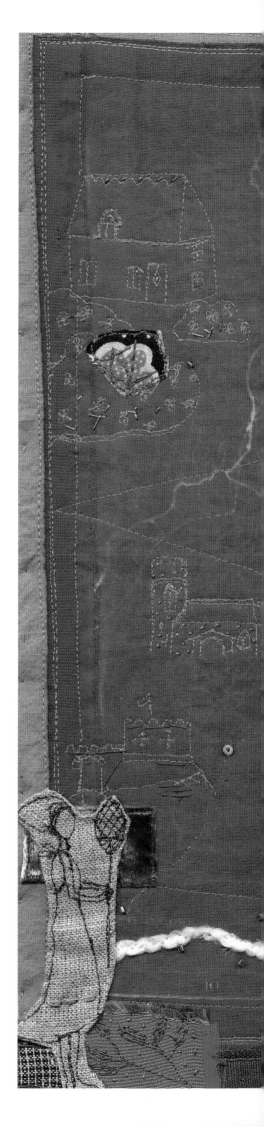

Michelle Holmes, Dawn Light Over the Suffolk Sea, 2012, cyanotype. Machine, hand stitching and applique on cotton, linen and velvet, 55 x 53cm.
Photograph by Terry Davies, reproduction of the artwork by kind permission of the artist

In Aldeburgh there has always been kinship with sailors from overseas, as long as they are not pirates or marauders. In January 1881, there were many nights of storms and floods, and several ships including a Russian steamer were driven ashore and wrecked. It had been a very cold winter with deep snow, ponds and streams iced over, and the beach and the marshes were thick with frost. On the nights of the 18 to the 21 January ferocious icy winds drove ships onto the sand-banks and on each night there were wrecks. The lifeboat was launched repeatedly and the people of the town watched freezing and unable to help from the shore.

On that occasion five unnamed sailors, whose bodies were washed on to the beach, were buried in a corner of the churchyard. This space has become known as Sailors' Corner and is kept for the bodies of unidentified victims of shipwrecks.

The treacherous sandbanks that lie off Aldeburgh beach are home to the wrecks of hundreds of ships lost in the this busy shipping route that leads down to London. The list of ships lost is long. In 1626 alone, the year after Charles I became King, Dunkirkers landed on the beach but they were driven away; ten ships were recorded as wrecked or taken by marauders: *The Mayflower*; *The Nightingale*; *The Hopewell* (twice); *Mary Magdalen*; *Jewell and George*; *Mary Ann*; *The Dragon*; *The Pilgrim*; *Ellen and George*; *Mary and John Speedwell*.

CHAPTER 13:

THE COASTLINE AND THE FUTURE

'If Dunwich is falling into the sea, will Aldeburgh go the same way?' That question has been asked every year since 1953, when terrible storms flooded the town and damaged many buildings. Nowadays we have become accustomed to stories of destructive flooding - not only in distant countries, but almost every winter in Britain. We are not immune. But Aldeburgh has survived many floods over the centuries of recorded history. In 1938 there was destruction on Crag Path and earlier in the century a number of storms finally swept the buildings of Slaughden and its famous quay into the sea.

Caroline McAdam Clark, Pagodas and Stony Ditch, Orford Ness, 2013, oil and pencil on paper, 18 x 28cm. Reproduced by kind permission of the artist.

The records of ships lost in the 1700s suggest that period to be the most destructive in the long battle between man and the sea. Indeed that century saw storms that straightened out the shoreline and washed away the two whole streets that lay to the east of the market square. Those streets are clearly present on Tudor maps, but there is no sign of them now.

Jonathan Trim, High Tide and Strong Winds,
Aldeburgh Beach, mixed media on paper.
Reproduced by kind permission of the artist.

Above and opposite:
Three photographs of the floods of 1953. The storms of 31 January 1953 ravaged the coastlines of Holland, Belgium and East Anglia. The river walls of the Alde were breached as the water levels rose and at least 307 people along the east coast of England died, and 24,000 homes were destroyed. In Aldeburgh there were no deaths that night, although one man later drowned whilst trying to repair breaches in the sea defences.
Photographs © the estate of Florence Fahnestalk, 1953, reproduced courtesy of Steve Fahnestalk.

Left:
The Three Mariners Inn at Slaughden was almost completely surrounded by flood water in 1907.
(From *Sophia's Son* by Dorothy Thompson, Terence Dalton Publishing, 1969)

The shingle spit of land that extends down to Shingle Street has been growing naturally for centuries. At this point the river Ore (the Alde becomes the Ore at Orford) turns finally and dramatically into the sea, leaving a desolate beachscape in front of the old Customs House and cottages.

Over the centuries the town has been both protected from, and exposed to, the sea. In the Middle Ages the beach eroded far enough for two streets to be removed along the Aldeburgh frontage, but at the moment the shingle beach acts as a defence as it accumulates in volume, which in turn provides greater protection. The beach is many feet higher, for example, in front of the Brudenell Hotel than it was only twenty years ago when the groins were visible and it was a long jump down from the wall of Crag

Sophie Macpherson,
Boat on Beach.
Reproduced by kind
permission of the artist.

198

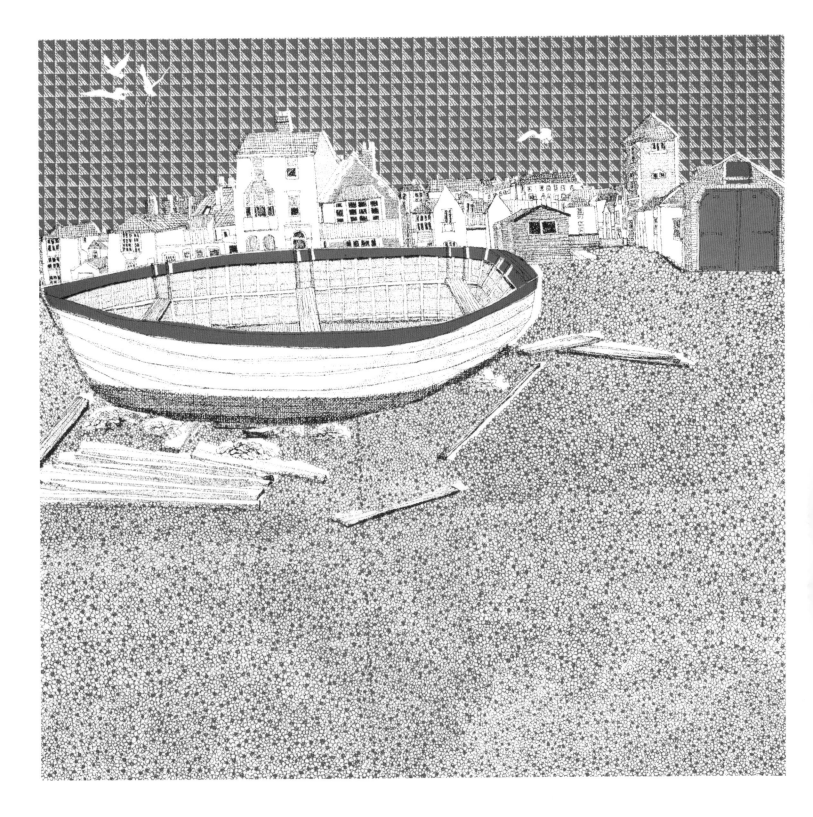

Clare Halifax, Beached Boat, silkscreen print, 22 x 22cm. Reproduced by kind permission of the artist.

Path onto the beach. As has always been the case, the channel between the shore and the sandbanks are what determines the flow of tide from north to south, and those tides create mighty and unpredictable forces.

In recent years new initiatives have developed in order to preserve and protect the Suffolk coastline and the valley of the river Alde. The Alde & Ore Association was set up in 1990 and through their River Defence Committee they act to monitor the river banks and provide early warning of possible problems. SCAR (Suffolk Coast Against Retreat) is a pressure group of local organisations and individuals who have come together to

call on the government to increase expenditure on protecting the Suffolk coast, in the belief that it 'should defend its people and coastal lands from flood and climate change as vigorously as from any other threat'.

In 2010 the Environment Agency published a Shoreline Management Plan to assess the environmental risks from the sea, and to suggest appropriate management regimes. In Aldeburgh and Snape Maltings the flood defence costs would be met by government

Shingle Street, where the river Ore, formerly the Alde, joins the sea. Photograph by Mike Page, reproduced by kind permission of the photographer.

funding, but other rural areas were not so fortunate. This has prompted the formation of a collaborative group of many interested parties around the estuary, supported by the Environment Agency and Natural England. The Alde and Ore Estuary Partnership has largely been delegated the power of decision over what happens to flood defences – provided that it can raise the cash. It is a large proviso, but what is certain is that this community-based approach to tackling these issues is at the heart of long-term thinking for the future of the Aldeburgh coastline.

POSTSCRIPT

For all its connections, Aldeburgh belongs to no one. Despite its famous town and district councils, burghers and bailiffs, no one rules over it. Its mayor does not pretend to be the voice of its public personality, as the Mayor of London might wish to be. It is not just a 'place where a music festival takes place' any more than it is just a 'seaside town in England'. 'Aldeburgh' is an area that includes Snape, the lost town of Hazelwood, the mysteries and buried treasures of Yarn Hill and Rendlesham Forest, if not Orford and Thorpeness and all the histories of those places, too. It is the land defined by the thirteenth-century Dutch drains and dykes in Snape priory. It is a long and ever-changing shingle beach. It is a manor without a manor house; a fort without a fortress. It is the view from the south of Slaughden ferry as Turner found it. It is a town with public monuments to Benjamin Britten and a small dog, Snooks, who accompanied the local doctor on his rounds and is fondly remembered by all, but almost nothing to Newson, Elizabeth or Millicent Garrett, who have had at least as much influence for good and for the town's wealth, health and spirit.

Aldeburgh is most certainly not just the town of Crabbe or Britten and Pears or even of the remarkable Garrett family, but it is also a place which tells by its scars, the history of the English Church and Civil War in remarkable and gruesome detail. And it is one of the glorious treasures of Tudor England in a way that has been forgotten and lost apart from the obvious history of the Moot Hall and in the borough coat of arms.

Even more than these things, the town of Aldeburgh is a group of families whose names recur from century to century and who can follow their own ancestry in the churchyards, the parish registers, the lifeboat records and the war memorials of the surrounding towns and villages. These are families, many of whom must have been here for 8,000 years since the new waters of the North Sea formed a line down the coast of Suffolk and people first took their boats out to sea to fish. They have been here since the time when people learned to read and write to describe their trading and their interdependency; since people began to paint and to enjoy music. They were experts at survival and subsistence in ways that we would envy. They absorbed invasions from Italy, Germany, Denmark, Holland and France and the proximate fear of attack from Dunkirk, from Spain, from Russia and from Germany again. Their community meant rescue, raising children, and survival from flood and storm. And for them, too, it always meant peaceful days in the land and seascape that are still as remarkable and to be enjoyed as ever they were.

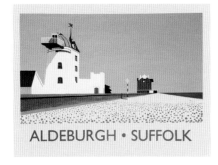

David Kirk, Aldeburgh Suffolk, from the 'Town Prints' series. Digital inkjet print, 2010, 45.5 x 64cm.
Reproduced by kind permission of the artist, courtesy of goldmarkart.com

Peggy Somervile, South Look-out, Aldeburgh, c.1960, pastel, 35 x 26cm.
Reproduced by kind permisson of the Somerville estate.

INDEX

'A Warning to the Curious' 99
Adès, Thomas 46, *46, 49*
airfield 168, 179
Albert Herring 37, 38
Alde House 146, 158
Alde, river 16, 42, 46, 57, 82, 90, 94, 102, 114, 123, 152, 166
Aldeburgh Bookshop 8, 16, 24
Aldeburgh Festival 10, 14, 16, 38-55, 57, 82, 130, 153, 202
    fire 44
    founding 26, 31-3, 38-40
    musical directors 49
    proms 52
Aldeburgh, The, lifeboat 184*, 185-7*
Aldringham 76, 150
Anderson, Elizabeth Garrett 155, 158-62, *158,* 165, 202
Anderson, Skelton 162
Anglo Saxon Chronicle 96
Auden, W. H. 28-29, *29,* 30, 31

Barber's Point 82, 88, 90, 94, *95,* 166, 169
Barnes, Rob *110, 112*
Barrie, J.M. 20, 71
Bawtree, John *16-17, 135*
Bence, Alexander (Squire) 123
Bentwaters, USAF 52, 179-81, *179*
Berkeley, Lennox 29
Bhadresa, Penny *147*
Bigod, Hugh, Earl of Norfolk 109, 167
Blackheath House 152
Blackwell, Elizabeth 159-60
Bleak House 132, 134
boat building 16, 90, 100, 111, 120
boatyards 16, 61, 76, 82, 104
Boleyn Anne 108, 110
Boudica 90-1, *91,* 94
Bowman, Amelia *149*
Brandon, Charles 103, *103*
Bridge, Frank 26, *26,* 29-30
Bridges, Alan *14, 15, 131*
Britten, Benjamin 8, 13, 26-55, *27,* 121, 123, 130, 143, 202
    centenary 55
    early life 26-30
    move to Suffolk 29, 33
    musical development 26-41
    Red House 8, *38,* 42, 43, 121
Britten, Beth 28
Brudenell Hotel 12, 22, *153,* 158, 168, 186, 198
Brudenell Terrace *153*
Buckingham, Duke of 168, 170
Burdett-Coutts, Angela 139, *139*
Burwood, Millie 135

Butley Priory 118
Cable, James (born 1851) 184-7, *185*
Cable, James (joined lifeboats 1954) 186
Cable, James (joined lifeboats 1998) 186
Carver, Jill *6-7*
Cassius Dio 91
Catchpole, Margaret 100, *109*
Chambers, Derek *2, 101*
Charles V of Spain 108
Churchyard, Thomas *60, 170, 190-01*
City of Winchester, lifeboat 182
Clodd, Edward 71-72, 74-75
Cobbold family 188-89
Colchester 54, 82, 90, 91
    abbey 116, 118-19
Collins, Wilkie 75
Cook, Willie 139
Cooke, Richard *52*
Copland, Aaron 30, 31
Crabbe, George 14, 24, 31-33, 36, 61, 68, *69,* 70-71, 75, 111, 132, 155, 202
crag, mineral stone 142
Crag Path 12-13, *15,* 72, 75, 132, *133,* 135, *135, 137,* 150, 194, 199
Cranbrook, Lady, 39
Crespigny House 57, 132, 142, *143,* 146
Cringle, Tom *63*
Crispe, William 113
Cross, Joan 36, 37
Crozier, Eric 36, 37, 38
Crusades *115,* 118
Curlew River 44, *123*
Customs House, The *71, 188,* 198

Davidson, Septimus 96
de Mersey, John 118-19
Death in Venice 54, 55
Deben, river 10, 96
Dickens, Charles 132, 134
Dodds, James *124, 125*
Donaldson, Ros *50-51*
Dougall, Helen *47*
Dowsing, William 125, 128
Drake, Sir Francis 16, 103, 104, *105*
Dunkirkers 104, 166, 167, 192
Dunwich 82, 88, 122, 154, 155, 194
Dyer, Emily 185

Eaton House 142
Edinburgh House 142
Edward VI, King 109
Edward VII, King 139, 142
Edwards, Laurence *84-5*
Elizabeth I, Queen 105, 111, 112, 122, 123

Elizabeth II, Queen 46, *49*
English Opera Group 37, 38, 39
Fahnestalk, Florence 196
Fass, Marjorie 29
Fawcett, Henry 162
Fawcett, Millicent 160, *161,* 162, *162,* 165, 202
Felixstowe 142, 148, 166
fish and chip shop 24, *25*
fishermen 10, 13, 61, 76, 88, 105, 110, 116, 119, 120, 122, 135, 139, 149, 158, 168, 189
    huts on the beach 22, *23,* 189, *190-1*
FitzGerald, Edward 10, 71
flood of 1907 *196*
flood of 1953 *196-97*
Fort Green 22, *24,* 168, *170*
Framlingham 109, 155, 166-7
    castle 166
    school 139
Friston Hall 135, 150

Garrett, Balls 153, 155
Garrett, Elizabeth (see Anderson)
Garrett, Louisa 154-5, 158-9, 160, 162
Garrett, Millicent (see Fawcett)
Garrett, Newson 12, 42, 44, 46, 54, 142, 153-62, *154,* 165, 184, 202
Garrett, Richard 137, 139, 145, 153
Garrett, Sarah (née Balls) 153
Garrett Iron Works 137, *138, 140-1,* 145, 153, 155, *164, 165*
George, Jules 8, *12-13, 20-21,* 24, *64, 65, 116, 172-3*
Gissing, George 71, 74
Glemham House 39-40
Glyndebourne 36-37, 38
Golden Hind 16, 104, *104, 105*
golf club 174
Green, Kenneth *33*
Griffith, Diane *98*
gun emplacement 22, 135, 171, *175*

Halifax, Clare *199*
Hall, Jennifer *38*
Halt, Lieutenant Colonel 180-81
Hambling, Maggi 44, *63*
Hardy, Thomas 71, 72
Hari, Kenneth *29*
Harvey, John 188
Haven, the 17, 20, 21, 82, 94, 99, 102, 104, 111, 112, 146
Hazelwood 10, *89,* 99, 114, 116, 139, 143, 152, 202
Henry VII, King 100
Henry VIII, King 100, 103, 108-10, 120-22

Hepworth, Barbara 57, 71
High Street 12, 24, 68, 71, 111, 132, *134*, 142, 178, 188
Hodgson, Heather *83*
Hoffman, Theronda *9, 18-19, 25*
Holmes, Michelle *73, 192-3*
Hopkins, Matthew 128, 130
Howard, Thomas, Duke of Norfolk 109, *109*, 122
Hudson's flour mill 29, *30,* 143

Iken 54, 90-91, 96, 114, 116, 174
Ionia, houseboat 76, *77*, 78
Isherwood, Christopher 29, 30

Laurance, Martin *177*
Laurent-Aimard, Pierre 49
Lay, Cecil H. *76, 80-1*
Leiston *74*, 94, 99, 137, 139, *140-1*, 145, 148, 153, 155, 158, 160, *164*, 170, 179, 188
   abbey *117*
   iron works (see Garrett Iron Works)
lifeboats 182-92
   disaster of 1899 144, 182, 186, *187*
lighthouse 146-7, *147*
Listener, The 32

Macpherson, Sophie *198*
Magdapur, SS 169
map *74, 95, 102, 168*
Marine Villa 150, 152
Marjoram the chimney sweep 142
Martel, William 116-8
Martello Tower 10, 16, 24, 57, 61, 82, 132, 134, 147, 170, *171, 172-3*
Mary Tudor 103
Mary Tudor (Bloody Mary) 110
Menuhin, Yehudi 36
meteorite 125, 126, 180
Millais, John Everett *75*
Moore, Henry 57
Moot Hall 8, 68, *70,* 82, 90, *101,* 102, *108*, 109, 111, 120, 130, 132, 139, 169, 187, 202
Morris, Elizabeth *126-7, 183*

Neill, A.S. 145
New English Singers 30
No Name 74-75
Norman, Chrissy *31, 56-7, 97, 136*
Noye's Fludde 40, *40,* 41

Omar Khayyam 71, *72*
Ore, river 198, *200-01*
Orford 10, 40, *41*, 57, 82, 90, 99, 112, 113, 116-118, 142, 158, 198
   castle 147, 167, *167*
   lighthouse 146, *147*
   Ness 82, 146, *147*, 167, *176,* 178, 186
Orlando the Marmalade Cat 76, 78

Packard, Edward 142
Page, Mike *42, 179, 200-1*

Pankhurst, Emmeline *162*, 165
Pead, Jack *184*
Pears, Peter 16, 29-32, 36-44, 46, 48-9, 52, 202
Peter Grimes 13, 32-3, *33*, 36, 45, 54, 63
pier 24, 148, 165
Piper John 36, *37,* 40, 45, *60, 121*
Polaine, Peter *99*
Potter Mary 42, *43*

Radford, Gary *70*
Raedwald, Anglo Saxon king 96, 98, 114, 167
railway 10, 74, 137, 145, 148, 156, 158, 169, 174, 179
Rape of Lucretia, The 36, 37
Rationalists, The 72, 74-5
Reekie, Jonathan 49
Rendlesham 180, 202
Rudling, Laurie *55, 180*

Sadler's Wells 33, 36
Sailors'Corner 192
salt extraction *88,* 88, 94
Saxmundham 10, 74, 82, 94, 142, 148, 168, 170, 174
Sea Interludes 13
Shingle Street 16, *113,* 175, *177,* 198, *200-01*
Sizewell nuclear power station 52, *53,* *144,* 145
Slater, Montagu 34
Slaughden 10, 16, 24, 57, 76, *77,* 82, 102, 103, 104, 109, 111, 118, 150, 155, 158, 165, 194, *196,* 201, 202
Slee, Colin *89, 119*
Sluice Cottage 17, 112
smuggling 20, 68, 142, 188
   Hadleigh gang 188
Snape 10, 29, 30, *30,* 38, *45,* 46, *62,* 76, 82, 94, *96, 98,* 99, 102, 109, 114, 116-7, 125, 135, 142, 155, 158, 166, 188, 202
   priory 116, 118-9, 120, 202
   racecourse 135-7
Snape Maltings 16, 29, *42, 48, 49,* 57, 143, 155, *156-157,* 200
   concert hall 36, 45, 46, *49, 52,* 55, 153
   construction of 29, 42, 45, 155, 158
   fire 45, *48,* 48-9
Snape Warren 137
Snooks the dog *3,* 202
Spanish Armada 104, *106-07,* 122, 150, 153
Speer, Cyndi *92-3*
Spice, Graham *113*
Spring-Rice, Margery, 40
sprats 120
St Augustine 96, 114
St Botolph 96, 114
St Peter and St Paul, church *40,* 96, *122,* 130
steam locomotive *138*

steam ploughing engine *159*
Strafford, Earls of (see Wentworth)
Strafford House 71, 150
suffragettes 162, *163*
Summerhill 145
Sutton Hoo 95-6, 98, 114

tank traps *174*
telegraph 146
Territorial Army 31, 170
Thames, river 83, 137
Theberton 169
Thellusson House 132
Thellusson, Peter 132, 134
Thomas, Glynn *44, 71, 207*
Thompson, Dorothy *76,* 142-3
Thompson, Georgina 139, 142, 152
Thompson, Rev. Henry 75-6, *76,* 139, 143
Thorpeness 16, 21, 22, 72, 99, 112, 169, 171, 174, 178
   Meare 20
Three Mariners inn 158, *196*
Thurlow, Dave *174, 175*
Tomlinson, Alex *178*
Topcliffe, Robert 75, 122-4, 128
Trim, Jonathan *44, 66, 67, 195*
Turner, J.M.W. 10, 57, 61, *58-9, 61,* 202

UFOs *178,* 179-80
Uplands 155, 158
University of Essex choir *52*

vikings 54, 82, 97, 98, 99, 166

Walden, Mandy *11, 22, 34-5*
Ward, Charles 184, 186
Washington-Dixon, Halima *86-7*
Watson, Malcolm *46, 54*
Wells, H. G. 71-2
Wentworth Hotel 142
Wentworth, Leveson Vernon 76, 143, 150, 152, 189
Wentworth, Thomas, First Earl of Strafford 150, *150*
Wentworth, Thomas, Third Earl of Strafford 150, *151*
White Lion Hotel 93, 139, 148
Whiteland, Mrs 179-80
William the Conqueror 98, 99, 116, 167
windmills 16, 61, 146, *146,* 174
witches 128-9, *129*
Wolsey, Thomas 102, 103, 108, 109, 120, 121, 122
Woodbridge 8, 10, 37, 52, 71, 82, 95, 96, 179, 180
Woods, Trevor *62, 144*
World War One 76, 135, 145, *165,* 168, 178
World War Two 16, 22, 46, 54, 130, 135, 169, *174, 175*

Yarn Hill 90, 202

Zeppelin airships 168-9, 179

SELECT BIBLIOGRAPHY

Anon. (1949) *Official Guide of the Aldeburgh Corporation*. Norwich, Norfolk: Jarrold & Sons.

Anon. [n.d.] *Aldeburgh: The Official Guide*. Various editions. Ipswich, Suffolk: F. W. Pawsey & Sons.

Anon [n.d.] *Aldeburgh-on-sea and District*. Shilling Guide series. London: Ward Lock & Co.

Anon. [n.d.] *Borough of Aldeburgh: the Official Guide*. Various editions. Carshalton: Home Publishing.

Arnott, W. G. (1961) *Alde Estuary: The Story of a Suffolk River*. Second edition. Ipswich, Suffolk: Norman Adlard & Co.

Bacon, J. & Bacon, S. (1984) Aldeburgh, Suffolk. Colchester, Essex: Segment Publications.

Bellingham, J. C. *et al.* [n.d.] Aldeburgh Festival programme, several editions. Snape, Suffolk: Aldeburgh Music.

Blythe, R. (1957) *The Parish Church of St Peter & St Paul, Aldeburgh, Suffolk*. Southwold, Suffolk: Southwold Press.

Blythe, R. (ed.) (1972) *Aldeburgh Anthology*. Aldeburgh, Suffolk & London: Snape Maltings Foundation, in association with Faber Music.

Bristow, J. P. (2000) *Aldeburgh Diary*. Third revised edition. Aldeburgh, Suffolk: Aldeburgh Museum Trust.

Burnet, E. (1968) *All Sayles Bearinge: An Aldeburgh Notebook*. Ipswich, Suffolk: Norman Adlard & Co.

Burwood, A. C. [n.d.] *My Seafairing Ancestors*. Private publication.

Carpenter, H. (2003) *Benjamin Britten*. London: Faber & Faber.

Carter, G. G. (1949) *Margaret Catchpole: The Girl from Wolfkettel*. London: Methuen.

Clodd, E. (1861) *A guide to Aldeburgh – with a brief description of adjacent places (being a handbook for visitors and residents)*. First edition. Aldeburgh, Suffolk: J. Buck.

Clodd, H. P. (1959) *Aldeburgh: The History of an Ancient Borough*. First edition. Ipswich, Suffolk: Norman Adlard & Co.

Crabbe, G. (1807) *Poems*. Project Gutenberg edition, 1 March 2004. Available at www.gutenberg.org

Crabbe, G. (1816) *Letter IX: Amusements*. In: *The Borough: A Poem in Twenty-Four Letters*. Sixth edition. London: J. Hatchard.

Daniell, W. (1822) *A Voyage Round Great Britain*, Volume VI: plate 221, The Orford Ness Lighthouses, Suffolk. In: Clodd, H. P. (1959) *Aldeburgh: The History of an Ancient Borough*. First edition. Ipswich, Suffolk: Norman Adlard & Co.

Dewing, G. (1995) *Aldeburgh 1939–1945*. East Molesey, Surrey: G. Dewing.

Dewing, G. (1998) *Air Station Aldeburgh 1915–1919*. East Molesey, Surrey: Geoff Dewing

Dutt, W. A. (1909) *The Norfolk and Suffolk Coast*. The County Coast series. New York, USA: Frederick A. Stokes.

Glynn, J. (2008) *The Pioneering Garretts: Breaking the Barriers for Women*. London: Hambledon Continuum.

Headington, C. (1996) *Britten*. The Illustrated Lives of Great Composers series. London: Omnibus Press.

Hele, N. F. (1870) *Notes or Jottings about Aldeburgh*. London

Hughes, D. (2008) *Aldeburgh Revisited: a Portrait of a Seaside Town*. Aldeburgh, Suffolk: Aldeburgh Museum (Moot Hall), in association with the Aldeburgh Bookshop.

James, M. R. (1925) *A Warning to the Curious and Other Ghost Stories*. London: Edward Arnold.

Maine, G. F. (ed.) (1947) *Rubaiyat of Omar Khayyam*. New edition. E. FitzGerald (trans.). London & Glasgow: Collins.

Manton, J. (1966) *Elizabeth Garrett Anderson*. London: Methuen.

Munn, G. C. (2006) *Southwold: An Earthly Paradise*. Martlesham, Suffolk: Antique Collectors' Club.

Neave, D. (1990) Saxmundham, Leiston and Aldeburgh Remembered In Old Postcards. Images Publications.

Pevsner, N. (1961) *Suffolk*. Buildings of England series. E. Radcliffe (rev.), 1974. London: Penguin Books.

Pipe, J. (1976) *Port on the Alde: Snape and the Maltings*. Snape, Suffolk: Snape Craft Centre, Snape Maltings.

Poster, J. (ed.) (1986) *Selected Poems, George Crabbe*. Manchester: Carcanet Press.

Potter, J. (1998) *Mary Potter: A Life of Painting*. Aldershot, Suffolk: Scolar Press.

Thompson, D. (1969) *Sophia's Son: The Story of a Suffolk Parson. The Rev. Henry Thompson, M.A., his life and times (1841–1916)*. Lavenham, Suffolk: Terence Dalton.

Trevelyan, J. [n.d.] *The Alde*.

Waddell, J. (2001) 'Snape's colourful history can be traced back for 2000 years'. Available at www.snapevillage.co.uk

Waddell, J., Taylor, P., *et al. Chronicle*, various issues1}. Aldeburgh, Suffolk: Aldeburgh and District Local History Society.

William Filmer-Sankey, W. & Pestell, T. (2001) *Snape Anglo-Saxon Cemetery: Excavations and Surveys 1824–1992*. East Anglian Archaeology report no. EAA95. Ipswich, Suffolk: Archaeological Service.

Winn, A. T. (1926) *Records of the Borough of Aldeburgh – The Church*. Hertford: Stephen Austin & Sons.

Glynn Thomas, Aldeburgh Boats, 2011, etching, 9 x 14cm.
Reproduced by kind permission of the artist.